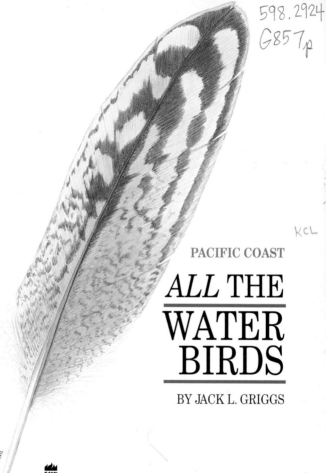

marbled godwit

PACIFIC COAST

ALL THE
WATER
BIRDS

BY JACK L. GRIGGS

HarperPerennial

A Division of HarperCollins*Publishers*

Designed by Jack L. Griggs & Peg Alrich
Edited by Virginia Croft
Illustrations reformatted by John E. Griggs
from the original illustrations published in
All the Birds of North America
by the following artists:

Jonathan Alderfer pp. 55-63, 69-87, 97-119;
John Dawson p. 120; Alan Messer pp. 65-67;
Hans Peeters pp. 89-95; Bart Rulon pp. 33-35;
Barry Van Dusen pp. 37-53.

All the Waterbirds: Pacific Coast

FIRST EDITION

Library of Congress Cataloging-in-Publication Data

    Griggs, Jack L.
        All the water birds. Pacific Coast / Jack L. Griggs.
           p. cm.
        Includes index.
        ISBN 0-06-273651-5
        1. Water birds—Pacific Coast (North America)—Identification.
    I. Title
    QL684.G775   1999
    598.176'0979—dc21   98-41933

99 00 01 02 03 ❖/PE 6 5 4 3 2 1

The **American Bird Conservancy (ABC)** is a U.S.-based, not-for-profit organization formed to unify bird conservation efforts across the Americas and dedicated to the conservation of birds throughout the Western Hemisphere. ABC practices conservation through partnership, bringing together the partners whose expertise and resources are best suited to each task.

The **ABC Policy Council** has a membership of more than 70 organizations sharing a common interest in the conservation of birds. Composed of ornithologists, policy specialists, educators, and general bird enthusiasts, the Council is a professional forum for exchanging information and discussing critical and emerging bird conservation issues. The Council provides policy and scientific advice to conservationists, stimulates a network of support for conservation policies through national, state, and local groups, and directly accomplishes conservation through ABC.

ABC is a working member of **Partners in Flight (PIF)**, an Americas-wide coalition of more than 150 organizations and government agencies dedicated to bird conservation. Initially begun to find ways to reverse the decline in neotropical migratory bird species, PIF has broadened its scope to include all non-game birds in the Americas. PIF links birders, hunters, government, industry, landowners, and other citizens in a unified effort to conserve bird populations and habitats.

Many North American "birds" found in this guide spend more than half their lives in Latin America and the Caribbean. The needs for bird conservation in this region are at least as great as in the U.S. Through PIF, ABC is building U.S. support for capable, but often underfunded, conservation partners throughout the Americas.

PIF's bird conservation strategy, called the **Flight Plan**, can be obtained from ABC, the National Fish and Wildlife Foundation, or the U.S. Fish and Wildlife Service. PIF's National Coordinator serves on ABC's staff, and ABC helps implement the Flight Plan through its Important Bird Areas (IBA) initiative. ABC members receive *Bird Conservation*, the magazine about PIF and American bird conservation.

Want to Help Conserve Birds?

It's as Easy as ABC!

By becoming a member of the American
Bird Conservancy, you can help ensure
work is being done to protect many of the
species in this field guide. You can receive *Bird
Conservation* magazine quarterly to learn about bird
conservation throughout the Americas and *World Birdwatch*
magazine for information on international bird conservation.

Make a difference to birds.
Copy this card and mail to the address listed below.

☐ **Yes,** I want to become a member and receive *Bird
Conservation* magazine.
A check in the amount of $18 is enclosed.

☐ **Yes,** I want to become an International member of
ABC and receive both *Bird Conservation* and
World Birdwatch magazines.
A check in the amount of $40 is enclosed.

NAME

ADDRESS

CITY/STATE/ZIP CODE

Return to: American Bird Conservancy
1250 24th Street NW, Suite 400; Washington, DC 20037
or call **1-888-BIRD-MAG** or e-mail: abc@abcbirds.org

Memberships are tax deductible to the extent allowable by law.

Contents

COASTAL BIRD HABITAT

by
EDWARD S. BRINKLEY

Coastal waterbirds spend their lives in a world dominated by the ebb and flow of tides, the movement of water masses in response to the gravitational pull of the moon and sun. Most people don't consider the tides when going out to see birds, but tides can make the difference between seeing many species and coming up empty-handed.

In all areas affected by tides, low or falling tides are critical feeding times for many coastal birds because their prey—small marine organisms— are exposed or covered by much less water, making them easier to hunt. An area of open water, devoid of bird life at one time of day, may be transformed into a mudflat teeming with shorebirds only a few hours later.

Knowing the difference between a falling tide, when shorebirds may feed in the strip of exposed mudflat nearest the shoreline (and nearest the observers), and lowest tide (when the shorebirds may be tiny specks scattered in the great distance across a huge mudflat) can also make a difference. Low tide in some places exposes shellfish beds of oysters or mussels, so that specialists like the black oystercatcher can begin to feed.

In some circumstances, falling tides create conditions (especially at river mouths such as that of the great Columbia River) that concentrate fish and other prey. Fish-eaters such as pelicans, gulls, terns, cormorants, loons, and grebes may gather in large aggregations at such times.

SUN

EARTH   or

MOON

SPRING TIDES

By contrast, high spring tides are sometimes the best time to search for those elusive chicken-like marsh dwellers known as rails. They are sometimes concentrated by the highest tides into the high, dry, and more exposed ends of a marsh. Usually rails skulk about unnoticed in a marsh's dense interior.

It helps to understand how tides work. Each day, largely because of the revolution of the moon around the earth, there are two high and two low tides, at least in most places. The moon's orbital speed also determines that there is a daily shift of about 50 minutes in the timing of the tides, so that if you know that one high tide is at 3:00 p.m. today, you can estimate that it will be around 3:50 p.m. tomorrow. Checking a local tide table is an excellent way to begin a coastal birding adventure.

SUN

MOON   EARTH

NEAP TIDES

If the sun is aligned with the moon and earth, the highest and lowest tides are created, called spring tides. When the sun and moon are at right angles with respect to the earth, tidal change is much smaller, and these are known as neap tides. These tidal cycles complete themselves every two weeks.

Tidal currents vary tremendously from place to place. In many places on the Pacific coast, especially in the Pacific Northwest, tides can be very powerful, with differences between high and low tide in some places as much as 20 feet! Such a strong surge means that in many places smaller particles of stone and sand are washed away from coastlines, leaving mostly rocks and pebbles.

ROCKY COASTAL SHORELINE

Much of the northern Pacific coast is rocky, whereas in southern California, white sand (calcite from finely ground shell) beaches predominate. From this softer, more pliable substance, the milder southern tides may create sandbars and small sand islands— wonderful places to observe resting birds.

The kind of substrate that makes up a shoreline or flat—mud, sand, or stone—determines what sort of organisms will be found there and thus also what birds.

The intertidal zone is the area between the high and low water marks. In the Coast Range region, from Canada south to California's San Rafael Mountains, this area is a dynamic and sometimes harsh environment that nevertheless supports a great variety of seaweed (species of algae) on the rocky shores. Within this vegetation, in tidal pools and on the rocks themselves, marine life proliferates. Species specialize at different levels of the intertidal zone, depending on the amount of time an area spends submerged at high tide.

Most of the animal life on rocky shores is enclosed in hard shells for protection—shellfish. Some, like the common red crab, are crustaceans (shellfish with segmented bodies). Crabs can move about and feed on whatever they find. They, in turn, are prey for gulls and the larger shorebirds. Some gulls regularly forage in the intertidal zone, especially at tidal pools, where they take small fish and many types of shellfish.

RED CRAB
to 7"

Some crustaceans, such as barnacles, attach themselves permanently to rocks or pilings, where they are savored by shorebirds such as the rock sandpiper. Wintering rock sandpipers are specialists on the rocks of the intertidal zone. They are scarce, however. Others, such as the wandering tattler, the surfbird, and the turnstones, are more numerous on rocks. They also probe among the algae and mussels for small louse-like crustaceans sometimes called "sow bugs" and for fish eggs and mollusks.

ACORN BARNACLE
to 1/2"

Mollusks are shellfish with unsegmented bodies. Some, like the blue mussel, have two parts to the shell—bivalves. Those with a single hard shell fall into many classifications, but almost all of them—limpets, periwinkles,

SOW BUGS
to 5/8"

11

BLUE MUSSELS
to 4"

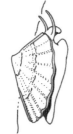

SHIELD LIMPET
to 1 1/2"

CHANNELED DOGWINKLE
to 1"

dogwinkles, chitons, and others—are eaten by shorebirds, gulls, and sea ducks.

Black oystercatchers, the only shorebirds that stay on rocky shores to nest, prey heavily on mussels. They use their long, scissor-like bill to snip the muscle that holds the mussel closed. Diving ducks such as the scoters devour mussels and other shellfish with less finesse. They swallow them whole and grind the shells in their gizzards.

Most sandpipers are found away from rocky shores, in the extensive silty mudflats exposed on coasts, marshes, and river mouths during low tides. Here sandpipers and plovers in countless shimmering masses come to feed on the variety of small marine organisms in the mud and shallow tidal pools. The bills of the different sandpipers are of varying lengths and shapes, so that all areas and levels of a mudflat are exploited.

Many of the tiny prey gleaned from the surface by small-billed birds like the least sandpiper are too small for an observer to see. Likewise, it is usually impossible to see the prey caught by the sandpipers that probe into the mud. Sometimes, however, a worm can be seen pulled from its burrow like a strand of spaghetti.

12

RED CHITON
to 1"

Marine worms such as clam worms and mud worms tunnel though coastal mud much like the familiar earthworm. They are a prolific source of food for shorebirds. The whimbrel is partial to large worms known as sipunculids. "Amphipods" are abundant on mudflats and rock pools. These are tiny crustaceans without hard shells that provide food for dozens of waterbird species.

Above the high water line, birds such as guillemots, murres, and cormorants nest in crevices between rocks and on rocky coastal cliffs along much of the coast. In areas of the Pacific Northwest where the ocean meets the shoreline directly, without the shelter of an island or a peninsula, the influence of the waves and tide is typically felt beyond the high water mark, as salt spray is tossed well back into coastal forests.

The open water beyond the low tide mark is where the majority of birds feed on the northern coasts. This is the area of coastline still affected by both tides and the influence of river systems but never exposed during low tide. In this environment, well within sight of shore, many varieties of birds forage. Some are aerialists that feed by picking from the water's surface or plunge-diving from flight. Others are swimmers that dive from the surface.

CLAM WORM
to 8"

Most of the aerialists feed on fish, but they also take morsels such as squid or shrimp that venture too near the water's surface. Small fish are also popular prey with surface divers such as loons, mergansers, and grebes. However, many swimmers, such as the scoters, eiders, and other sea ducks, dive for mussels and similar shellfish that attach themselves to pilings and rocky bottoms.

In the case of cormorants, the substrate of the ocean floor makes a difference: double-cresteds, which pursue fish in shallower waters, usually feed over sandy bottoms, while Brandt's and pelagic cormorants, which more often extract slow-moving prey from between rocks, hunt mostly over rocky bottoms.

Just offshore there are often tidelines or rips visible, areas where outgoing tides have con-centrated flotsam along distinct, winding, foamy lines. One type of shorebird, the phalarope, has adapted to foraging along these areas, where planktonic organisms are concentrated. Large groups of both red and red-necked phalaropes can sometimes be seen feeding in these areas, along with Bonaparte's gulls and sometimes black-legged kittiwakes.

Species that dive for fish are also usually present along tidelines if currents are strong enough. Kelp beds are present in relatively sheltered areas offshore, and several species of gulls and terns forage on the small fish and other marine life they attract.

The intertidal zones of more southerly sandy beaches are generally narrower, only a few yards wide in some places, but even here the resident organisms must cope with periods of immersion and exposure. Birds find an abundant variety of prey on which to feed at low tide, including beach hoppers (sand fleas), mole crabs, and various-sized clams.

SAND FLEA
about 1"

Mole crabs are the familiar oval-shaped, inch-long or smaller creatures found constantly burrowing back into wet sand after being exhumed by waves. They and their larvae are important prey for gulls and especially shorebirds, from the large whimbrel to the little sanderlings.

MOLE CRAB
to 1"

Beach hoppers or sand fleas are not fleas but amphipods (small crustaceans without shells) that live on the drier portions of a beach. Plovers often scamper after them. Clams, including the small tellins, are food for even the smallest shorebirds. They are captured in the wet sand when the clams' bodies are extended outside the open shell.

TELLINS
to 1/2"

In the winter months, gulls can often be seen in the intertidal zone with the shorebirds, either feeding or loafing (waiting until the next feeding period).

Above the intertidal zone on sandy beaches along the entire coast, one finds lines of jetsam called wrack. Birds such as the ruddy turnstone and snowy plover forage in the wrack for beach hoppers, flies, beetles, and any small organisms that have washed up. Gulls, which feed opportunistically on dead or dying fish and crabs that wash ashore, sometimes inspect the wrack line.

Wrack lines also attract crows. In fact, the Northwestern crow could be considered a waterbird if not for its landbird lineage. Considered by some a separate species from the widespread American crow, the Northwestern crow specializes in feeding along shorelines from Puget Sound northward and is the only crow on these coasts.

Snowy plovers and least terns are the only species that nest in the dry sand above high water line. Both are declining and threatened by loss of undisturbed nesting habitat. They remain largely in protected sanctuaries on southern California military installations, the last areas free of beachgoing humans.

Off the beaches, over the coastal waters bordering California's Transverse and Peninsular

Ranges, one sees a great diversity of waterbirds over the changing seasons. Numerous species of terns and the brown pelican plunge-dive for fish. The brown pelican can be seen in great numbers along beaches from about Humbolt Bay, CA, to the border with Mexico. Foraging pelicans are often attended by large numbers of Heermann's gulls, which harass the pelicans into giving up fish!

In winter, black-vented shearwaters can be easy to see from headlands south of Santa Barbara, such as La Jolla and Rancho Palos Verdes. Astonishing concentrations of loons, grebes, and ducks (largely scoters) can be observed in winter and during migration from the central coast beaches, and it is common to see various species of geese and dabbling ducks also migrating off the coast, even though they do not forage in the deep water here.

In spring and early summer, oceanic foragers like the sooty shearwater and the parasitic jaeger can sometimes be seen from shore. Numerous other seabird species may be observed with a telescope (and patience) from shore—or, better still, by taking a trip to the offshore waters where they live.

**PARASITIC JAEGER
CHASING TERN**

It isn't necessary to go far offshore. Monterey Bay, CA, which unlike most bays is fairly open to the ocean and fully marine, attracts whales and numerous oceanic birds. They, in turn, attract many nature watchers. Albatrosses, jaegers, shearwaters, phalaropes, and auklets are there to be seen.

Hunting for fish along the coast isn't limited to seabirds. Fish-eating raptors such as ospreys and the bald eagle are seen more and more often along the beaches, especially in the Pacific Northwest. Their populations, like those of the brown pelican, were severely reduced by pesticide poisoning in the 1950s and 1960s, but numbers of all three species continue to rise in the 1990s.

adult

young

BALD EAGLES

Bald eagles are well known for their white heads and tails, but young birds have dark heads and dark-banded tails. Ospreys can be recognized in flight at a good distance by their wing shape and bold underwing pattern. The wing shape is gull-like. Note how the leading edge of the wing projects forward at the wrist, unlike the wings of the bald eagle or other raptors. The projection is emphasized by the black patch at the wrist contrasting with the white underbody.

OSPREY

In late fall migration, watch for falcons, especially the peregrine falcon and the merlin, as they course high overhead or zip low along the coast hunting small shorebirds or coastal migrants such as swallows and warblers.

MERLIN

PEREGRINE FALCON

Because they fly so fast, falcons can be hard to identify without experience. Their flight, swift and direct, is a helpful mark. The gleaming white breast of the peregrine (tinged with cinnamon in some western birds) is a good mark. The merlin's color varies with sex and region, but all are streaked below and have a dark tail with pale bands and a whitish tip.

Coastal headlands tend to concentrate migrating songbirds and may hold over a hundred species present along the immediate coast in the fall migration—many of which are only in brief transit on their way to wintering grounds to the south (see *All the Birds of North America*).

Sheltered inlets and bays occur where rivers, streams, and creeks flow into the ocean. These coastal areas are not exposed to the open ocean and the beating of the waves. Some of the most diverse and bird-friendly habitats develop in these estuaries.

Estuaries are the areas where rivers and streams meet the ocean. The mixture of freshwater and saltwater masses makes for a unique environment of low-salinity water called brackish water. (Monterey Bay is fully marine, in contrast to the bays considered here.) Extensive marshes often form near the river mouths and on the borders of bays, and because high tides push marine water well up into the river, these are known as tidal marshes or salt marshes.

SHRIMP LARVAE
to 1/4"

Lagoons are similar to estuaries but are more cut off from tidal exchange. They may be brackish, with sufficient inflow of fresh water, or highly saline (salt pans) if evaporation is rapid. Stilts frequent salt pans along the coast of California.

Lagoons, estuaries, and protected marshes can hold great abundances of small marine life, including both adult and larval forms of many insects, worms, snails, clams, oysters, shrimp, jellyfish, sea slugs, and more. This bounty attracts a wide variety of waterbirds during most times of year.

CRAB ZOEA
to 1/8"

Salt marshes are limited in extent along the California coast from about Humboldt Bay south. They have been much reduced by human activity. Four species depend on salt marshes for nesting: clapper and black rails and savannah and song sparrows.

Other birds that nest in nearby habitats, such as kingfishers, prefer the quiet waters of marshes, rivers, and estuaries to the ocean waters. Forster's terns, which nest in the vicinity, are also likely to be seen coursing over marshes hunting insects and small fish.

HARRIER

Birds most at home on fresh water, such as the white pelican, blue-winged teal, pied-billed grebe, and green heron, may be found here in winter as well.

Raptors also frequent prey-rich marshes. During the day, harriers (once appropriately named marsh hawks) hunt rodents over marshes; at dusk, with luck, a barn owl or short-eared owl may be seen hunting the same prey in a similar fashion.

SHORT-EARED OWL

Foraging style is a helpful mark for harriers. They fly low and buoyantly over marshes with wings in a shallow V, hunting rodents by sight and sound. The females are brown above; the males, gray. Both sexes have distinctive white rumps that are easily seen.

The barn owl's heart-shaped facial disc is distinctive. The white or cinnamon underparts are good marks also. Short-eared owls are a tawny brown with dark marks at the bend of the wings visible in flight. The "ears" are seldom visible; the head appears round.

BARN OWL

The observer who watches the taller marsh vegetation patiently may be rewarded during migration or in winter with views of a sora or a Virginia rail. If even taller vegetation such as small trees is available next to the marshes, snowy and great egrets, great blue herons,

21

or black-crowned night-herons may nest in colonies and feed in the marshes. Each species feeds in a slightly different area or depth of marsh on slightly different species or sizes of fish, and some, like the night-herons, at specialized times of day.

In migration and through the winter, a great variety of shorebirds makes use of salt marshes and their related tidal pools, mudflats, and guts (the narrow open waterways in a salt marsh). These shorebirds feast on organisms similar to those found in open mudflats, but salt marshes also provide seeds and aquatic vegetation, which most shorebirds also take in small amounts.

Waterfowl are the primary consumers of aquatic vegetation, however, and the protected coastal waters of the Pacific are home to millions of geese, swans, and ducks over the winter season. With patience and luck, many of the native species of waterfowl can be observed in a small area of bay and marsh and adjacent ocean in just a morning's outing!

Swans, geese, and dabbling ducks such as the mallard, pintail, and the various teal stay closer to shore as a rule, because they feed by "tipping up" in shallow waters to graze on bottom vegetation. Diving ducks like the

TUNDRA SWAN DABBLING

redhead, bufflehead, goldeneyes and scaup are often called "bay ducks" for their preference for deeper, more open water. Some diving ducks graze on vegetation from deep bottoms, and many more forage for marine animals along the bottom. Because marsh and bay are sometimes so close together, it is often possible to watch dabblers and divers at the same time.

Brant (dabbling, duck-sized geese) are closely tied to salt-marsh habitats with abundant eelgrass and similar aquatic vegetation. In areas with damaged ecosystems, brant and other such specialists have been greatly reduced in numbers.

Bays and river mouths, too, are often home in winter to a whole host of grebes—western, Clark's, horned, eared, and pied-billed. In some protected bays of the Pacific Northwest, tundra swans and trumpeter swans may be plentiful.

Several bird-watching sites along the Pacific coast are so special they deserve specific mention. At Monterey, boats that take bird-watchers offshore (mostly on weekends) have recorded more species of oceanic birds than in any other place in North America. The entire Monterey Bay and Monterey peninsula from Moss Landing to Point Piños can provide outstanding opportunities to see shearwaters, jaegers, alcids, and other oceanic birds. Pigeon Point, San Mateo County, CA, is another excellent place to watch the ocean for birds.

To the north, San Francisco Bay is much more sheltered and so is home to more marsh dwellers, including rails, and to dabbling ducks. Large rafts of diving ducks can be found in the deeper waters. Nearby Golden Gate Park is a good place to study bay and ocean birds up close, as well as a good variety of landbirds.

Farther north, in Marin County, some of the West's best birding is to be found in a triangular area between Olema, Tomales Point, and Point Reyes Peninsula. Here there is open ocean (try Chimney Rock at Point Reyes), bays (Bodega and Tomales Bays), and much estuarine habitat with extensive mudflats and marshes. This mix of habitats means that there is a patch here for just about any waterbird.

Coos Bay, OR also attracts vast numbers of birds. At North Spit, terns, gulls, and shorebirds can be found. The small sloughs nearby can teem with thousands of shorebirds, egrets, and dabbling ducks. For the best ocean watching, try Cape Arago.

Seattle, on the vast Puget Sound, can be very birdy! Right in the downtown area, pigeon guillemots nest in the docks, and in the colder months, Barrow's goldeneyes feed on mollusks clinging to old pilings while marbled murrelets and many species of grebe bob nearby. Alki Point with its rocky shoreline attracts tattlers, surfbirds, oystercatchers, even harlequin ducks! Lake Washington holds flocks of dabbling ducks, and West Point (Discovery Park) is well known as a great sea-watch spot.

Coastal ecosystems are fragile. Between the ceaseless and very complex interactions of freshwater and saltwater environments along the coastlines, millions of waterbirds make their living. They are able to anticipate the rhythms of the coast's ecosystems and thus can locate the optimal feeding places and times with unerring accuracy.

Many species return as migrants, nesters, or winterers to precisely the same beach or marsh where they spent the previous season —or, in some cases, where their ancestors foraged thousands of generations before.

It is a sad fact of modern life that the 20th century's population explosion in North America has made areas of coastline more and more desirable and more densely developed and populated than at any other time in history. Fragile coastal environments have been altered, with any number of consequences, mostly negative, for birds and other wildlife.

Bulkheads that provide a perch for gulls, terns, and cormorants may mark the former site of a lush salt marsh. Rock jetties may change the pattern of beach erosion in some places for better or for worse, but they have turned out to be beneficial for some birds, particularly those that require rocky habitats—species such as rock sandpipers, Brandt's cormorants, and pelagic cormorants can often be found on such structures.

Likewise, dredge-spoil islands, the by-products of creating deeper channels for ship traffic and deeper harbors, marinas, and anchorages, have become havens for nesting terns, as these artificial islands mimic the natural barrier islands and bars created by tidal activity.

But these cases are exceptional: beaches, marshes, and estuaries have been destroyed and developed for human settlement extensively, especially in southern California. Very little pristine coastal habitat survives outside protected areas.

It is hoped that users of this guide will remember the fragility of coastal environments they visit, tread lightly and respect their inhabitants, and support local efforts to preserve the health of North America's coasts.

HOW TO LOOK AT A WATER-BIRD

AERIALISTS

SWIMMERS

WADING BIRDS

SHOREBIRDS

The way birds feed and their adaptations for feeding are the most important points to recognize in identifying and understanding them. For the beginner, the color and pattern of an unknown bird can be so striking that important points of shape and behavior go unnoticed. But feeding adaptations, especially bill shape, best reveal a bird's role in nature—its truest identity.

Waterbirds use one of four general strategies for catching prey. There are aerialists, swimmers, wading birds, and shorebirds. The sole exception is the kingfisher. Birds that use the same general strategy resemble one another, and the differences between birds that use different strategies can be recognized at a distance without binoculars.

The aerialists, such as gulls and terns, fly on long, slender wings, scanning the water and shores below in search of food. Some simply pick prey or scavenge from the surface. The magnificent frigatebird picks while in flight and seldom even gets its feathers wet. Other aerialists plunge-dive rather than pick. They search for fish swimming close to the water's surface and attack by folding their wings and plunging headfirst into the water below. The gannet plunge-dives from heights of 25 feet or more.

The swimmers, such as ducks and cormorants, search for food from the water's surface. Some dive to chase fish or feed from bottoms that can be 100 feet below the surface. Others, like geese and the ducks known as dabblers, don't dive but feed from the surface or tip up to graze on vegetation growing on shallow bottoms. The grazers also take vegetation at the water's edge. Some geese travel to nearby croplands to feed on grains and growing plants.

The swimmers have wide bodies for floating on the water; most have webbed feet. Their profile on the water is very different from that of a resting gull, and their flight is swift and direct, not at all like the slow, searching flight of the aerialists.

The wading birds and shorebirds pursue their prey on foot. The wading birds, such as herons, stalk through marshes and wetlands, often capturing prey such as fish, frogs, and crabs with a sudden thrust of a dagger-like bill. Nearly all except some elusive rails are large birds with long legs and heavy bills.

Shorebirds typically probe for small marine organisms on the mudflats, beaches, and rocks of the intertidal zone. Their bills are slender for efficient probing. The larger shorebirds and some of the smaller ones, too, have remarkably long bills (check out the curlews on p. 100).

Note that shorebirds often wade, and wading birds can be seen on mudflats and marsh edges with shorebirds. Because they both stalk prey on foot, the larger shorebirds and the wading birds have many similarities—long legs, long necks, and elongated bodies. Bill shape is a good structural mark for separating them. Also note that herons can fold their necks and often do; shorebirds can't.

In this guide, the waterbirds are grouped by their four general foraging styles. Within each group, birds are listed by size, the larger birds first. Birds of similar size and shape usually have distinctive plumages, but a few species closely resemble one another and must be identified carefully.

Young birds, seen in summer and fall, often have a different plumage than adults, but each is the same size and shape as the adult. Any young bird that has a plumage confusingly different from the adult's is illustrated. Some young birds molt to adult plumage in their first fall, but many take longer. Large gulls wear distinctive immature plumage until they are three or four years old.

Most names used to describe parts of a waterbird are fairly predictable—back, crown, bill, etc. "Mantle" and "speculum" are not as obvious. Mantle refers to the back and adjoining wing areas, which are often the same color. The speculum is the bright patch on the trailing edge of a duck's wing, near the body. Many ducks, including all the dabblers, have speculums, which are useful identification marks.

HOW TO READ THE MAPS

Range maps provide a simplified picture of a species' distribution. They indicate the birds that can be expected at any locality. Birds are not evenly distributed over their ranges. They require suitable habitat and are typically scarcest at their range limits. Some birds seem scarce because they are secretive.

Many birds that live on the coast for most of the year migrate inland or to the Arctic to nest. A few species that live elsewhere are seen on our coasts only in migration. Spring migration can last until mid-June for some species. By early July a few of the earliest nesters (usually the unsuccessful ones) are already winging it south. For shorebirds, spring migration peaks in April and May; fall migration, in August and September.

MAP KEY

SUMMER OR NESTING

WINTER

ALL YEAR

MIGRATION
(spring & fall)

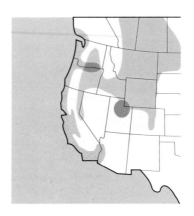

THE BIRDS

Not all ducks are called ducks—eider, teal, and scaup, for instance, are also ducks. In the list below, birds with names different from their common group name are listed in parentheses following the group name.

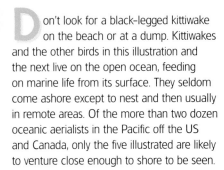

PARASITIC JAEGER

BLACK-LEGGED KITTIWAKE

Pomarine jaegers migrate offshore like parasitic jaegers but are seldom in sight of land. They are larger and bulkier than the parasitic jaeger, and the adult's tail streamers are twisted and blunt tipped instead of pointed.

on't look for a black-legged kittiwake on the beach or at a dump. Kittiwakes and the other birds in this illustration and the next live on the open ocean, feeding on marine life from its surface. They seldom come ashore except to nest and then usually in remote areas. Of the more than two dozen oceanic aerialists in the Pacific off the US and Canada, only the five illustrated are likely to venture close enough to shore to be seen.

In winter, kittiwakes spread from the shoreline to about 100 miles out. Individuals nearest the shore are often young birds. Kittiwakes are numerous in cold, northern waters, scarcer to the south. They feed primarily on small fish, swallowed whole.

Adult **black-legged kittiwakes** have wing tips with a distinctive "dipped-in-ink" look. There are no white spots in the black. The black markings on young birds are also distinctive.

Jaegers are muscular, predatory cousins of gulls. They fly solo and often pirate the catch of other seabirds. Some **parasitic jaegers** migrate near shore in spring and fall. Plumage varies considerably, but the white flash in the dark wing is a good mark. The pointed tail streamers are excellent marks but are absent in young birds and can be missing in adults.

32

dark form

young

Parasitic Jaeger

pale form

Black-legged
Kittiwake

young

winter

FULMAR

BLACK-VENTED SHEARWATER

SOOTY SHEARWATER

Salt glands near the base of the bill filter excess salt from the blood of oceanic birds, allowing them to drink seawater and live on the ocean.

The shearwaters, which include the fulmar, have the nostrils on their bills enclosed with tubes and are often called tubenoses. The name shearwater refers to their characteristic flight style: gliding close to the water on stiff wings with an occasional series of shallow wing beats, arcing up over ocean swells, and disappearing into the troughs.

Fulmars are rare in sight of land, although in some winters they visit harbors and bays, usually flying alone. They are bulky, with bull necks and bulging foreheads. Most on the Pacific are dark, but they can be pale or in between. The overall shape and the stout, yellow bill with prominent nostril tubes are good marks.

The most abundant tubenose and the one most often seen in summer from the coastline is the sooty shearwater. Huge flocks sometimes plunge-dive for fish just beyond the shoreline surf. **Sooty shearwaters** are dark (sooty) overall except for a paler underwing area.

In fall and winter, from Mexico north to Monterey Bay, **black-vented shearwaters** occur regularly within sight of land. The smallest Pacific coast shearwater, they glide less and flap more than other shearwaters. Their upperparts are dark brown blending to white below. They nest on islands off Baja California.

34

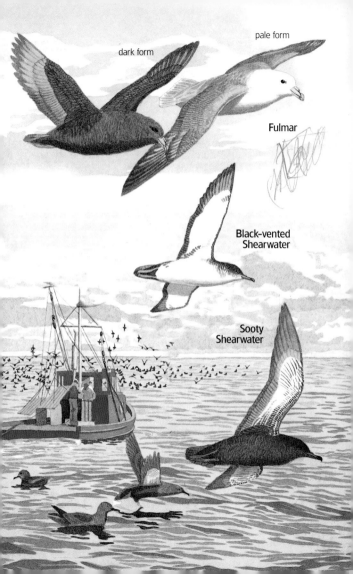

dark form

pale form

Fulmar

Black-vented
Shearwater

Sooty
Shearwater

BROWN
PELICAN

Decimated in the 1960s by pesticides, brown pelicans are now fairly numerous on the California coast, often looking for handouts at piers and marinas. In late summer and fall, a few wander as far north as Oregon and Washington.

The brown pelican makes dramatic plunge-dives amid schools of fish, using its huge bill and throat pouch to scoop them up. The dive is a spectacular ballet move performed by a clown. It is especially impressive when performed in sequence by a group of pelicans flying single file along the shoreline. When prey is spotted, the pelican banks steeply until it stalls in flight. Falling like a stone, the bird twists its body (but not its head) a half turn so that it smacks the water with its back. Underwater, the long, narrow lower beak and throat pouch stretch into a hoop-shaped net and scoop up the stunned fish.

White pelicans (p. 54) do not fly in search of prey and then plunge-dive like brown pelicans. White pelicans do their hunting from the water's surface, while swimming.

In winter, an adult **brown pelican** has a bright yellow head and white neck. The head fades to white in summer, and the hind neck becomes a dark reddish brown. Young birds in their first year have a dark brown head and neck and a white belly. In their second year, young pelicans become grayer above and darker below. Adult plumage is attained in the third year.

36

White Pelican
p. 54

winter

Brown
Pelican

summer

1st year

WESTERN GULL

GLAUCOUS-WINGED GULL

Brownish gulls are young birds. They are illustrated on p. 46.

Western, glaucous-winged, and herring gulls are opportunistic feeders. Many take live prey from the ocean's surface far from the shoreline. They also scavenge on coastal tide flats and at landfills.

The six large white-headed, adult gulls in this and the following two illustrations should be compared with one another. The herring gull in the next illustration is nearly the size of the western and glaucous-winged gulls. When seen in mixed flocks, the remaining three are noticeably smaller.

Other than western gulls, only a very few white-headed gulls—those that choose not to migrate and nest—remain on shores south of mid-Oregon in summer. Throughout the rest of the year, western and glaucous-winged gulls are numerous; herring gulls are scarcer. Note the dark streaks on the white heads and necks in winter. Many western gulls on the California coast stay white-headed year-round.

The **western gull** has a distinctively darker mantle than either the herring or glaucous-winged gull. **Glaucous-winged gulls** lack the black in the wing tips of both western and herring gulls. However, identification is complicated because western and glaucous-winged gulls commonly interbreed, producing offspring that can look similar to herring gulls. Hybrids are especially common on Washington and northern Oregon shores. A good mark for either parent or hybrids is the heavy bill, slightly swollen at the tip.

38

Western
Gull

western

example of
glaucous-
winged and
western hybrid

glaucous-
winged

winter

summer

Glaucous-winged
Gull

GULLS

HERRING GULL

CALIFORNIA GULL

Another gull, closely resembling the herring gull but much scarcer, is found on the Pacific Coast in winter—Thayer's gull. Identifying one is a job for experts. The most visible mark is in the wing tip, where the adult Thayer's shows less black, especially on the underwing, than the herring gull does.

alifornia gulls are much more numerous on the Pacific than herring gulls. Some California gulls remain all summer. Both gulls are found in virtually all shoreline habitats and range inland and out over the ocean.

The previous account (p. 38) describes how to distinguish the herring gull from western and glaucous-winged gulls and their hybrids. The herring gull is almost the size of those gulls; California gulls are smaller, although larger than the two white-headed gulls that follow. Don't be confused by the herring gull being about the same size as the California in the illustration. It is shown at a bit of an angle, foreshortened. The same illusions happen in real life bird-watching. Size can be an uncertain mark.

Better marks for separating adult **California** and **herring** gulls are mantle color, leg color, eye color, and the shape and color of the bill. Mantle color is the best mark at a distance. The California gull's mantle is darker than the herring's, and its legs are greenish yellow (adult) or dull blue-gray (sub-adult). The bill of the California gull is more slender and has a black mark as well as a red spot, although a very few herring gulls can show a black mark. Up close, note the California's dark eye. Also compare the California gull with the ring-billed and mew gulls that follow.

summer

Herring Gull

California

winter

herring

herring

California

summer

California Gull

winter

MEW GULL

RING-BILLED GULL

Another useful mark for standing gulls is the white crescent that appears on the backs (below the midpoint) of some. It is called the scapular crescent and can be seen on mew gulls and California gulls. Ring-billed gulls don't have one.

The ring-billed and mew gulls are the smallest of the six similar white-headed gulls on the Pacific coast. They are present most of the year, but in summer they migrate inland or to the Arctic to nest.

Ring-billed gulls have increased in numbers steadily since the 1920s and now are considered a pest in some areas. They are the most likely gull to be found scavenging at shopping malls and coastal fast-food franchises. They also feed extensively on small fish that school close to the ocean's surface.

Mew gulls are most common on northern coasts. They can be scarce on the shores of southern California. Like ring-bills, they scavenge in large numbers at harbors, piers, and landfills in winter.

Ring-billed gulls and **mew gulls** have yellow (or yellowish) legs, as does the California gull (see previous illustration). The larger white-headed gulls all have pink legs. The short, slender bill is a good mark for the mew gull. In winter, its bill is often greenish and sometimes shows a faint, dusky ring suggesting a ring-billed gull. Adult ring-billed gulls always have a pure yellow bill with a distinct black ring. At close range, eye color is a good mark. Mew gulls have dark eyes; ring-bills, yellow.

42

mew

ring-billed

ring-billed

Mew Gull

summer

winter

Ring-billed
Gull

summer

winter

onaparte's and Heermann's gulls are well marked and not likely to be confused with other gulls.

Bonaparte's is the smallest Pacific coast gull. Its black hood is a sure mark in spring before it migrates to nest in the north. When it returns in fall, the hood is gone or going. Only a smudgy dark spot remains on the side of the white head along with some pale gray on the hind crown and near the eye. The smudge spot is a reliable mark, however; so is the very slender black bill. In flight, note the Bonaparte's distinctive wing tip pattern.

Bonaparte's gull is fairly numerous from fall to spring along the entire coastline. Heermann's gull is also fairly numerous but not as widespread. It is primarily a Mexican species that wanders north in good numbers along the coast in summer and fall. Some can be seen on southern California coasts year-round.

The black-tipped red bill is a good mark for the adult **Heermann's gull,** but compare with the red-billed terns that follow. Also, note the distinctive gray breast and belly. In flight, the white-tipped black tail is easily seen. Many visiting Heermann's are dark young birds or winter adults with gray head streaks. The black legs and feet are useful marks for all.

BONAPARTE'S
GULL

HEERMANN'S
GULL

Another coastal bird with a black-tipped red bill is the black skimmer. A few live on California coasts just north of Mexico.

Black skimmers are black above and white below, but the most notable mark is the upper bill, which is distinctly shorter than the long lower bill.

44

Bonaparte's

summer
Bonaparte's

winter

Heermann's

Bonaparte's Gull

young

summer

Heermann's Gull

winter

YOUNG GULLS

When everything else on the beach has been identified, try your hand at the young brown gulls. All the brownish gulls with a dark band on their tails are young birds.

It takes four years in the larger species for a young gull to attain the smooth gray and white plumage of an adult. Ring-billed and mew gulls mature in three years; Bonaparte's in just two. At each molt (twice a year), their appearance changes. The youngest birds, in their first-winter plumage, are the darkest and have dark eyes. The plumage color lightens each spring and fall until adult plumage is achieved.

Young birds are the same size as adults, and size is a good clue in a mixed flock. Identify the adults, then match the young gulls with them by size when possible. Next, check the bill shape. Bill shape is the same in young birds as in adults, although size can vary individually.

Bill and plumage markings are the final points. Note the dark-tipped bill of the first-winter ring-bill. The ring forms by the second winter. Young California gulls also have dark-tipped bills but are browner, with less white in the tail. The dark tip of the first-winter herring gull's bill blends to a pale base. By second winter, its bill shows a ring, but plumage is darker than the second-winter ring-bill's, especially on the tail.

Typically there will be as many or more young gulls (one to three years old) on a beach as there are mature gulls, which can live twenty years or more. And perhaps half the young birds will be in their first year. The proportions of the age groups reveal the story of early mortality in gulls.

46

Bonaparte's Gull

Mew Gull

Ring-billed Gull

Herring Gull

Western Gull

Glaucous-winged Gull

2nd summer

3rd winter

California Gull

ALL STANDING BIRDS 1ST WINTER

TERNS

ELEGANT
TERN

CASPIAN
TERN

Royal terns from Mexico also visit southern California coasts, primarily in fall and winter. The royal tern has a heavier (and usually more orange) bill than the elegant tern. The black cap of the royal is more reduced in summer than the elegant's, leaving the dome and the area around the eyes white.

Terns look different than gulls, although the two are closely related. Terns are more slender and streamlined; most have pointed bills, long pointed wings, and forked tails. Although the Caspian tern approaches the size of a gull, most terns are smaller. The black cap is a good mark for a tern; most wear them throughout the summer.

Terns behave differently than gulls too. They don't interrupt their wing beats to glide on the shore breeze, as gulls often do. A tern strokes almost continuously, often cruising 10 or 20 feet above the water with its bill pointed down as it scans for small fish. Terns often hover over suspected prey, then plunge headfirst to capture it, something few gulls ever do.

Its bulky body and heavy red bill distinguish the **Caspian tern.** The dark wing tip (underside) is a good mark for flying birds. Black caps are streaked with white in young birds and winter adults. Caspian terns are fairly numerous in summer and fall. In winter, they withdraw south.

The **elegant tern** has a very slender yellow–orange bill. The forehead is usually white in summer and fall, when birds from Mexico wander north along the California coast. Since 1959 a few elegant terns have been nesting south of Los Angeles.

48

elegant

peak breeding

nonbreeding

Caspian

summer

winter

elegant

Caspian

peak breeding

Elegant Tern

young

young

Caspian Tern

summer

TERNS

COMMON
TERN

FORSTER'S
TERN

Arctic terns migrate well offshore in spring and fall. They are numerous, but rarely seen from the coastline.

In flight, the best mark for the arctic tern is subtle: its narrower, longer, sharply defined black trailing edge on the underwing. Their short necks give arctic terns a slightly different profile.

maller than the Caspian and elegant terns shown on the previous page, Forster's and common terns also sport black tips on their red or orange bills in summer. At least adults do. A young bird in summer looks similar to the winter adult; both have all-black bills.

Both Forster's and the common tern are numerous during migration in spring and fall. In winter, only Forster's tern remains in the US. Note its distinctive eye patch and the plain shoulder (the common tern has a dark shoulder bar in fall and winter). In migration, Forster's and common terns can be difficult to separate, even with binoculars.

One of the first clues in migration is habitat. **Forster's** prefers marshes, where it preys on large flying insects more often than fish. The **common tern** prefers plunging for fish near shore. However, both species are comfortable behaving like the other. Bill color is also helpful but not a certain clue. The bill is typically more orange in Forster's. In flight, the outer surface of the upper wing is a good mark. It is paler (frosted looking, some say) than the mantle in Forster's; a small dark wedge is visible in the common. When the bird is standing, the long forked tail of Forster's is a useful mark. It extends beyond the folded wing tip in Forster's, but not in the common tern.

common

Forster's

summer

summer

winter

winter

common
(late summer)

Forster's

summer

Common Tern

young

winter

young

summer

**Forster's
Tern**

winter

LEAST TERN

BLACK TERN

Since the 1960s, the black tern has been seriously declining. Flocks of several hundred migrating birds once were fairly commonplace. Now such a flock is rare.

The cause of the decline is uncertain, but damage to the nesting habitat is suspected.

The least and black terns are the small-est, scarcest, and most endangered of the terns. Least terns are summer visitors that prefer to nest on sand beaches or shell banks above the high water line. They have been displaced from most such sites by people. Many least terns now attempt to nest on a variety of substitute sites, including gravel rooftops, sand and gravel pits, even parking lots. The most successful substitute nesting sites have been islands of dredge-spoil waste in bays.

The least tern prefers fishing in shallow water. When it sights a fish, it often hovers above it before plunging. Least terns are most often seen singly, just offshore from ocean beaches and in bays and inlets. The small size is one good mark for the **least tern;** the yellow bill with black tip is the clincher. Also note the patch of white on the forehead.

Black terns nest in the interior and winter south of the US, but a declining number migrate along the Pacific coast, especially in fall. They frequently gather in flocks and can be seen flying offshore or feeding on insects over coastal marshes. Adult **black terns** are obvious in spring plumage, but their head and underparts are white in winter, and in fall migration some are molting and look patchy.

least

summer

winter

black

least

black

summer

fall (molting)

young

summer

Least Tern

young

summer

Black Tern

SWANS AND PELICANS

TUNDRA SWAN

TRUMPETER SWAN

WHITE PELICAN

Trumpeter swans were hunted until only a few thousand birds remained, most along the coast of British Columbia. They are now protected, and numbers are increasing.

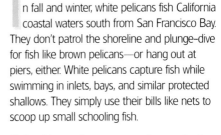

In fall and winter, white pelicans fish California coastal waters south from San Francisco Bay. They don't patrol the shoreline and plunge-dive for fish like brown pelicans—or hang out at piers, either. White pelicans capture fish while swimming in inlets, bays, and similar protected shallows. They simply use their bills like nets to scoop up small schooling fish.

It's hard to sneak up on prey when you're the size of a white pelican. Pelicans solve that problem by fishing together. Through coordinated movements, they herd small schooling fish toward each other or into shore. **White pelicans** are distinctively large and impressive.

Most trumpeter swans winter north of the US-Canadian border; most tundra swans winter to the south. Both birds are primarily vegetarians, using their long necks to reach plants several feet below the water's surface. Bays and inlets that provide good foraging are where they congregate in winter.

The **trumpeter swan** is larger than the tundra and has a deeper call. Note how the black skin encloses more of the trumpeter's eye. **Tundra swans** nearly always show a yellow spot before the eye and have a slightly dished bill. Young swans are gray-brown; their black bills and legs are marked with pink.

young

Tundra Swan

Brown Pelican
p. 36

young

Trumpeter Swan

tundra swan

White Pelican

WHITE-FRONTED GOOSE

SNOW GOOSE

Small numbers of Ross' geese can occasionally be found on the California coast, often with flocks of snow geese.

Ross' goose looks like a small white-form snow goose but has a stubbier bill, lacks the "grinning patch," and often shows purplish color at the base of the bill.

he white-fronted goose is scarce in winter in coastal habitats. It sometimes grazes on marsh vegetation but more often is seen on nearby and inland fields. The name refers to the small white band above the bill. Another mark for the adult **white-fronted goose** is the dark speckled belly. Legs are usually orange; the bill is usually pink, but these colors vary. Flocks fly in Vs and give a high-pitched, two-noted, "laughing" call. Escaped domestic geese can be mistaken for white-fronted geese.

Snow geese are fairly numerous in the coastal marshes of the Pacific Northwest. Flocks are scarcer on the California coast, where they prefer the marshes of the interior valleys.

Western flocks of snow geese sometimes include dark-form birds known as blue geese (illustrated in flight). There are also intermediates. The white head is a good mark for all adult **snow geese**. Also note the dark "lips" or "grinning patch" where the cutting edges of the bill meet. Young snow geese show some gray; the young blue goose is dark-headed and has a dark bill and legs.

In flight, snow geese bunch in undulating lines, earning them the popular name "wavies." The black wing tips resemble those of a white pelican (p. 54), which also flies in flocks.

domestic goose

young

White-fronted Goose

white-fronted

blue goose form of snow goose

Snow Goose

young

BRANT

CANADA
GOOSE

In fall migration,
most black brant fly
nonstop from their
Arctic coastal nesting
grounds to their
wintering sites along
the Pacific coast.

Few people need an introduction to the **Canada goose.** The black stocking-like head and neck and the white chin strap are familiar throughout the continent. Even flocks flying in the distance are recognized by the V-formation flight and resounding honks. There are many races in the West, some barely larger than a mallard and weighing as little as 3 pounds, others 3 feet long and weighing as much as 15 pounds.

Canada geese are primarily grazers. Along the Pacific coast, some winter on marsh grasses and other vegetation (especially north from Vancouver, B.C.), but most live inland. In parts of the Pacific Northwest, golf courses and grassy areas attract flocks that now stay year-round and have become pests.

Brant are grazers also, but they won't eat just any vegetation; they specialize in eelgrass. In shallow saltwater bays and inlets where eelgrass is plentiful, brant are often numerous.

Pacific coast brant have black bellies and are known as **black brant**. They are small geese and may be confused with ducks. On the water, they look dark overall until they tip up to feed and display their bright white rears. At close range, a small, stylish, white collar design can be seen on the neck of adults.

58

black brant

Brant

brant

Canada

Canada Goose

large race
with white neck ring

giant race

small race:
cackling goose

RED-THROATED LOON

PACIFIC LOON

COMMON LOON

Loons propel themselves underwater by their webbed feet, as do the cormorants shown in the next illustration. On land, loons are awkward.

oons usually sit low in the water instead of bobbing on top like some ducks. Because they dive for fish, loons can't be lighter than water or they couldn't submerge efficiently. They float on the surface by filling internal air sacs and by capturing air in their feathers.

All three loons are fairly common near shore or in protected deep-water bays and inlets in winter. Pacific loons are regularly seen in flocks, and common loons gather in flocks at night.

Bill shape is a good mark for loons. On the **red-throated loon,** the bill is slender and slightly upturned. The bill of the **Pacific loon** is straight and wider at the base. The **common loon** has the heaviest bill, and the lower mandible is angled up near midpoint.

In summer plumage, the necks, heads, and back patterns of the three loons are different. However, the more commonly seen winter plumages resemble one another. The best winter plumage mark is the pattern of dark and white on the side of each species' head and neck. On the red-throated, the white foreneck blends to the dark hindneck smoothly. The edge is sharper and closer to the foreneck on the Pacific loon, and there is usually a faint chin strap. On the common loon, white meets dark in a jagged line on the lower neck.

60

summer

winter

Red-throated Loon

red-throated

winter

Pacific Loon

summer

Pacific

young

Common Loon

winter

summer

CORMORANT

DOUBLE-CRESTED CORMORANT

BRANDT'S CORMORANT

PELAGIC CORMORANT

The throat skin is a flexible pouch for holding fish. It is similar to, but much smaller than, the pouches that pelicans have.

A large dark bird seen standing near the water with its wings spread is probably a cormorant. They dive for fish and, afterward, spread their wings to dry. Most diving birds have waterproof plumage, but the outer portion of the cormorant's plumage is wetable.

For cormorants, field marks are subtle. The double-crested has orange skin on the throat and in a line between the eye and the bill. Brandt's throat skin is blue in summer, but the better, year-round mark is the buff plumage patch bordering the skin. Brandt's is the only Pacific cormorant that commonly feeds in large flocks. For pelagic cormorants, the smaller size and more slender shape—especially of the head and neck—are good marks. Note the white flank patch in breeding plumage.

In flight, cormorants can sometimes be separated without binoculars. The **double-crested** holds its head above the body centerline and shows a distinctive kink in its neck. **Brandt's** flies with its neck straight or nearly so; there is often a slight bend near the base. The **pelagic cormorant's** neck is straight and very slender, with no visible head bulge as in the other two.

Cormorants show wispy white plumes on their heads and necks in spring and early summer, most prominently on the double-crested.

62

early summer

young

winter

double-crested

Brandt's

pelagic

Double-crested Cormorant

young

Brandt's Cormorant

winter

early summer

young

winter

early summer

Pelagic Cormorant

COMMON MURRE

PIGEON GUILLEMOT

Alcids "fly" underwater with their wings and use their feet as rudders for maneuvering.

The dark bar on the white wing patch of the pigeon guillemot distinguishes it from its Atlantic relative, the black guillemot.

The birds in this illustration and the next are alcids, duck-like oceanic birds that come ashore only to nest. Unlike the oceanic aerialists (pp. 32-34), alcids hunt their prey —mostly fish—underwater. They are often seen swimming between dives. Only a few alcid species are regularly seen from shore. The common murre and the pigeon guillemot are two that can be seen year-round.

In summer, huge numbers of common murres nest at a few widely spaced, dense colonies on offshore islands and rocky cliffs. They are more widespread in winter, alone and in flocks, ranging from far offshore to close in. The size and shape of the **common murre** are distinctive, especially the long slender bill. In summer, the head, neck, and breast are a deep brown.

Pigeon guillemots (*GILL-la-mots*) usually feed near shore, often in sheltered rocky areas in water less than 50 feet deep. They are typically seen singly or in pairs. Most nest on offshore islands, but they are versatile. Some nest in crevices on mainland cliffs, and they have been known to nest under wharves. In winter, guillemots are less often seen.

The white wing patch on the black upperwing is a good mark for the **pigeon guillemot** year-round. The legs are bright red.

winter

summer

murre

Common Murre

winter
guillemot

summer
guillemot

winter

summer

Pigeon Guillemot

**RHINOCEROS
AUKLET**

**MARBLED
MURRELET**

The tufted puffin nests primarily in the Arctic, but there are small nesting colonies south to northern California.

In summer, tufted puffins have huge orange bills, white faces, and long eyebrow tufts. Winter birds resemble the rhinoceros auklet but have much larger bills.

Like the alcids in the preceding illustration, the rhinoceros auklet and marbled murrelet live on the ocean and come ashore only to nest. Most rhinoceros auklets nest in a handful of colonies on islands from southeastern Alaska to Washington, although there are small colonies off Oregon and California. In winter, most birds are off the California coast and in protected areas like Puget Sound, WA.

The **rhinoceros auklet** is named for the pale horn on the yellow bill in summer. The bill is duller in winter, and the white head plumes are absent; the bird is dull gray-brown above with a pale belly and underwing seen in flight.

Marbled murrelets are scarce south of Canada. They are usually alone or in family groups, often in bays and inshore waters, where they dive for fish. In summer, **marbled murrelets** are a mottled brown above. In winter, the white stripe back from the shoulder is a good mark.

Marbled murrelets nest high in mature conifers as far as 30 miles inland. They are seriously declining because of the loss of coastal old-growth forest. Both the murrelet and the auklet typically fly to and from their nests just before dawn and at dusk to avoid predators like hawks and some gulls.

winter

summer

Rhinoceros Auklet

auklet

murrelet

young

summer

winter

Marbled Murrelet

SHOVELER

MALLARD

Most ducks have a distinctive patch of feathers known as the speculum along the trailing edge of the wing near the body. The speculum is typically brightly colored and is a useful identification mark for most species.

Along the coast, shovelers and mallards are numerous from fall through spring in shallow protected waters. They nest inland in summer. They won't be seen on deep water; they are not diving ducks but dabblers—ducks that feed from the surface or tip up to feed on bottom vegetation.

The male **shoveler's** colors are similar to the male mallard's, although arranged somewhat differently. Plumages of the two females are much alike. However, the outsized bill and long, sloping forehead give the shoveler—male and female—a very distinct look. Males have black bills (not yellow, as in the mallard); females have an orange edge to their dusky bills.

The bill is specialized for straining tiny aquatic animals from the water, and the shoveler is often seen swimming low in the water with its bill submerged. In flight, shovelers show green speculums (see sidebar) and blue wing patches. They often feed in small groups in winter.

Although the male **mallard** is distinctive, many female ducks resemble the mottled-brown female mallard. Her best marks are her bill, tail, and speculum. The bill is orange with a black saddle mark on top, the tail is mostly white, and the speculum is bright blue with white borders.

68

Shoveler

♀

♂

1st winter ♂

shoveler

mallard

Mallard

♂

tipping up

♀

downy young

GADWALL

PINTAIL

AMERICAN WIGEON

Rarely in a flock of American wigeons it is possible to see a Eurasian wigeon. The male Eurasian wigeon has a red-brown head and a buff crown; its sides are gray. Females are very much like American wigeons.

Gadwalls, pintails, and wigeons are dabbling ducks like mallards. They are primarily seen in winter on the Pacific coast, although some nest near portions of the coast in summer. Look for them in marshes, bays, or inlets in winter.

Gadwalls are numerous along the Pacific coast. They are usually seen in small flocks, often with pintails. The male **gadwall** is a finely detailed gray–brown. Look for the black rear end and the contrast of the brown head with the gray body. The female suggests a female mallard, but note the white belly and the gray bill with orange edges. Both sexes have a distinctive white speculum.

The **pintail** is fairly numerous along much of the coast. It would be hard to mistake a male. Females resemble other brown females. The white belly is a useful mark, but the longish bill, rounded head, and long slender neck are the best marks. The profile of the neck, head, and bill is a reliable mark for many ducks.

Note the short bill of the **American wigeon.** Male wigeons are bright, with a white or creamy forehead; females, brown with a grayish head. The green speculum (see sidebar, p. 68) and white shoulder patch (grayish in females) are good marks in flight.

70

gadwall

wigeon

Gadwall

♀ ♂

Pintail

♂ ♀

American Wigeon

♂ ♀

CINNAMON
TEAL

BLUE-WINGED
TEAL

GREEN-WINGED
TEAL

Teal and most ducks
molt all their flight
feathers at once a few
weeks after nesting.
At this time the birds
are especially vulner-
able. Males wear a
concealing "eclipse"
plumage resembling
the female's.

Teal are the smallest dabbling ducks. They often feed in small groups, dabbling for seeds and other tiny plants and animals in the shallow water stirred up by their swimming. All can be found in winter and during migration on portions of the Pacific coast in marshes, shallow bays, and protected inlets.

Green-winged teal are the most abundant and widespread teal along the Pacific coast. They often gather in large flocks. Cinnamon teal are fairly common. Blue-winged teal are scarce; most winter south of the US and migrate inland.

Like most dabbling ducks, male teal are bright and distinctive. It is the females that can cause identification problems. They are much alike when seen swimming—small and mottled brown, with dark bills. However, females usually associate with males of the same species.

The best confirming marks for a female are the size of the bill and the color of the forewing. Bills come in three sizes; small (green-winged), medium (blue-winged), and large (cinnamon). **Blue-winged teal** have blue forewings, and so does the **cinnamon teal**. But the **green-winged teal** doesn't have green forewings; it has a green speculum, like other teal. Its forewing is gray-brown like its body.

72

Cinnamon Teal

♂
♀

cinnamon

blue-winged

Blue-winged Teal

♀
♂

green-winged

Green-winged Teal

♀
♂

RING-NECKED DUCK

LESSER SCAUP

GREATER SCAUP

So why is it called a ring-necked duck when the ring is on the bill? Because with the bird in hand, a faint purple-brown collar can be seen. The name was given when bird-watching was done with a gun.

Scaup and ring-necked ducks dive to feed on bottom vegetation and aquatic life such as mussels and barnacles. From fall to spring, they range the length of the coast from Canada to Mexico. Scaup often form large flocks ("rafts"), usually over deep water.

Ring-necked ducks are scarce on salt water, but they do accept brackish inlets. They can dive 40 feet, but like scaup, they usually feed in shallower water. In very shallow water, they tip up like dabblers.

The white bill ring is a good mark for the **ring-necked duck.** At a distance, the white sides and black back are sufficient for identifying males. Scaup have gray backs. In the female, note the thin white eye-ring and pale eye line.

Scaup are difficult to separate. Females also closely resemble female ring-necks and red-heads (p. 76). The **lesser scaup** has a slightly smaller bill and a more peaked head; the **greater scaup's** crown is more rounded. Male greater scaups have grayer backs; females can show a pale spot on the side of the head in fall and winter not seen in most lesser scaup. In flight, both scaup show a white band on the trailing edge of the upper-wing. On the lesser scaup, the band turns gray on the outer wing.

74

Ring-necked Duck

♂ ♀

ring-necked

Lesser Scaup

♂ ♀

lesser

greater

Greater Scaup

♀ ♂

REDHEAD

CANVASBACK

RUDDY DUCK

Most diving ducks propel themselves underwater with their webbed feet. For efficient diving, the legs are placed well back on the body, so far back that some, like the ruddy duck, struggle to walk on land.

Canvasbacks, redheads, and ruddy ducks are divers that feed primarily on bottom vegetation. From fall to spring, they flock in coastal bays and marshes. Canvasbacks and redheads often gather in mixed flocks.

The male canvasback has a black breast and a chestnut head and neck like the redhead, but its back and sides are nearly white compared to the gray-bodied redhead. Best mark for the **canvasback**—especially the female—is the long, slightly dished bill and forehead.

Redheads have a fairly steep forehead and a rounded head. The bill is average sized and tipped with black. Female redheads are very much like the female scaup shown on the previous page; they are closely related. Female redheads are a tawnier brown than scaup and don't show white at the base of the bill, although the area near the bill may be pale.

Ruddy ducks usually keep to themselves in small, loose groups. Their small size and stiff tails give **ruddy ducks** an unusual look. The tail is often cocked at a 45-degree angle. For males, the white cheeks are good marks in summer and winter. Winter males lack the bright blue bill and chestnut plumage. Females have gray cheeks divided by a darker brown line.

redhead

canvasback

♀ ♂

Redhead

♀ ♂

Canvasback

Ruddy Duck

summer ♂

winter ♂

♀

**HARLEQUIN
DUCK**

BUFFLEHEAD

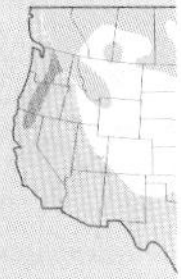

Harlequin ducks do
have accidents and
suffer broken bones
because of their
dangerous environ-
ment. In most cases,
the breaks mend and
the birds survive.

uffleheads and harlequin ducks are divers that feed primarily on shellfish. Buffleheads live on coastal bays, inlets, and harbors in winter. They are sometimes seen over shellfish beds in the open ocean beyond the breakers, but generally prefer protected waters. They are often seen singly or in small groups and are quite active.

The **bufflehead** is the smallest diving duck. Note the puffy head that inspired the bird's name. The steep forehead and short bill are also helpful marks. For males, the large white head patch is a prominent mark. Females are much duller overall but have a distinctive small white cheek patch. Flying birds resemble the goldeneyes in the next illustration.

It is difficult to imagine how harlequin ducks survive in the turbulent surf of the jagged, rocky coasts that they inhabit. When not feeding, they gather on shoreline boulders. Most summer on swift mountain waters.

The **harlequin duck** is small and chunky with a short bill, steep forehead, and rounded head. Males usually appear very dark overall with a bizarre assortment of white spots and stripes. In females, the white spots below and before the eye can merge or be indistinct, but the white ear spot is always sharp.

78

Harlequin Duck

♂

♀

harlequin

bufflehead

♀

♂

Bufflehead

COMMON
GOLDENEYE

BARROW'S
GOLDENEYE

Oldsquaws, a numer-
ous duck in the Arctic,
are occasionally
seen as far south as
northern California in
winter. They are
divers seen both in
bays and beyond
the breakers.

The oldsquaw's com-
plex plumage pat-
terns include black
patches at the rear of
the face in winter. The
best mark for males
is a pintail nearly as
long as the body.

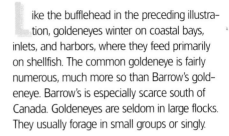

ike the bufflehead in the preceding illustration, goldeneyes winter on coastal bays,
inlets, and harbors, where they feed primarily
on shellfish. The common goldeneye is fairly
numerous, much more so than Barrow's goldeneye. Barrow's is especially scarce south of
Canada. Goldeneyes are seldom in large flocks.
They usually forage in small groups or singly.

Goldeneyes have puffy heads like the bufflehead (p. 78). The color and pattern of the
plumages of all three birds are also similar. A
good mark for the male **common goldeneye**
is the white spot before the eye. The male
Barrow's goldeneye has a white crescent.
At a distance, Barrow's dark "shoulder bar"
extending toward the water line is a good mark.
The head sheen is green in the male common,
purple in the male Barrow's, but under field
conditions, the heads often appear flat black.

Both females have brown heads, narrow white
collars, and bright yellow eyes. They are best
distinguished by head and bill shape; note the
steep forehead and stubby triangular bill of
Barrow's. Bill color is also a helpful mark.

In flight, goldeneyes show subtle differences
in the pattern of white in their wings. The
birds are sometimes called whistling ducks or
whistlers for the sound made by their wings.

80

♀   ♂   **Common Goldeneye**

Barrow's   common

♂   ♀   **Barrow's Goldeneye**

BLACK
SCOTER

SURF
SCOTER

WHITE-WINGED
SCOTER

Pigeon guillemots
(p. 64) in summer
plumage are also
dark, but their white
wing patches are
prominent even
when the birds
are swimming.

coters are diving ducks seen in bays and off the open shoreline along the Pacific coast in winter from Canada to Mexico. They often raft together in large numbers over shell-fish beds. Surf scoters are the most numerous; black scoters, the least; but concentrations of each species vary along the coast.

Scoters are dark. The coot (p. 84) is also dark, and other swimmers can appear dark in poor light. The male **black scoter** is the darkest. It has a distinctive orange bulb on its bill; females are browner and have a large whitish cheek patch. In flight, black scoters can be separated from surf scoters by the silvery patch on their underwings. Scoters fly close to the water, often in long strings.

Male **surf scoters** have the most distinctive head markings. The white spots are less pronounced on the head of the female but are still useful identification marks. The head and bill shape is a good mark as well.

On the water, the wing patch of the **white-winged scoter** is often hidden. However, the white around the eye of the adult male can be seen at a distance. Note the differences in head shape of the white-winged and black scoters and how far the feathering extends down the bill of the white-winged.

82

Black Scoter

♂ ♀

black

surf

Surf Scoter

♂ ♀

white-winged

White-winged Scoter

♂ ♀

RED-BREASTED
MERGANSER

COOT

CLARK'S AND
WESTERN GREBES

Grebes rarely fly
except in migration,
and then usually at
night, unseen.

Mergansers are diving ducks that feed primarily on fish rather than shellfish or vegetation. Their bills have serrations for holding the slippery prey. The shaggy crest and white collar distinguish the male **red-breasted merganser** from other mergansers. On females, note that the rusty head and upper neck blend smoothly to gray below. (On female common mergansers, a freshwater bird, the meeting line is sharp.) Red-breasted mergansers are numerous in winter, both off beaches and in protected bays and harbors.

Coots are more closely related to rails (p. 94) than to ducks. Nevertheless, they swim like a duck and associate with ducks. On coasts in winter, they range from brackish and salt marshes to protected bays. They feed from the surface and by diving, taking whatever they can catch. The **coot** is a dark bird like a scoter (p. 82) but has a chicken-like ivory bill.

Bill color and face pattern are slightly different in **Clark's** and **western grebes.** Clark's has the brighter, orange-yellow bill, and its eye is set in white, not black or gray, as in western grebes. Both are larger than the grebes shown on p. 87, with longer necks and bills. Clark's and western grebes are often in mixed flocks on sheltered coasts and inlets in winter; westerns typically far outnumber Clark's.

♀ ♂ young molting ♂

Red-breasted Merganser

Coot

Clark's Grebe

Western Grebe

typical

gray

EARED GREBE

HORNED GREBE

RED-NECKED GREBE

The pied-billed grebe is primarily a freshwater bird, but some are found in winter on brackish or salt water. It resembles a coot (p. 84) with its stubby, chicken-like bill but is brownish in winter and has dark eyes.

rebes look something like small ducks, but the families are not closely related. Grebes are almost always seen on the water, as they never come onto dry land. Nests are built in marsh vegetation. When startled, they don't fly but rapidly dive. Hell-diver is one of their common names. They dive for food—small fish, tiny shellfish, aquatic insects—and also pick morsels from the water's surface.

Grebes winter on coasts, both in protected bays and beyond the breakers. In winter, the different species look similar, patterned in shades of black and white. **Eared grebes** in winter are darker than the others, with a dirty-looking face and neck. The thin, slightly upturned bill is also a good mark. Eared grebes are more numerous than horned or red-necked grebes.

Horned grebes and red-necked grebes usually feed solo or in small groups. The **horned grebe** has a crisp neck pattern similar to that of the much larger western grebe shown on the preceding page; its head has a flatter crown than that of the similar-sized eared grebe. **Red-necked grebes** are larger than horned grebes. Most have a distinctive white throat strap in winter, but the heavy yellow-based bill is a safer mark; it is much larger than the bills of the two smaller grebes.

summer   winter

Eared Grebe

winter   summer

Horned Grebe

Red-necked Grebe

young   summer   winter

GREAT BLUE
HERON

**GREAT BLUE
HERON**

Great blue herons are widespread from Mexico to Alaska year-round on the Pacific coast. Many retreat from northern coasts in winter, but a few hardy individuals survive the subzero temperatures and winter storms of coastal Alaska. Most great blues feed in marshes, but they will forage anywhere there is something edible. Fish is their favorite prey, and they have been known to wade belly-deep into the surf stalking them.

The stately great blue typically wades slowly or waits patiently in shallow water for fish to approach. With a rapid thrust of its bill, it spears prey that ventures too close. Great blue herons often feed alone, but they are also seen with other herons.

Like other herons, great blues nest and roost in trees for protection from predators. Nesting colonies are often near the shoreline and can include a variety of herons, egrets, and other wading birds.

The **great blue heron** is so large that it is sometimes thought to be a crane. Sandhill cranes are rarely seen along the coast in migration. They have naked red foreheads, not the black head plumes and neck stripes of the great blue. A good mark at a distance is the way the neck is held. A heron's neck folds, and its head often rests on its shoulders. The neck can also be extended like a crane's, but usually a kink is apparent where the neck folds. In flight, the neck is always folded. The illustration shows the great blue as it takes off, before its neck is fully folded; the kink is evident.

88

sandhill crane
(shown for comparison)

Great Blue Heron

young

WHITE
HERONS

**GREAT
EGRET**

**SNOWY
EGRET**

Plume hunters
destroyed entire
colonies of nesting
egrets at the end of
the 19th century, dis-
rupting even the
nesting of species
they were not hunt-
ing. Opposition to the
wanton killing coa-
lesced into the
Audubon movement,
which brought the
era of millinery
slaughter to an end.

gret is another name for heron. The name comes from the long, showy white plumes, "aigrettes," on the necks and backs of some herons in breeding plumage. These plumes, prized adornments for women's hats at the time, led to the birds' slaughter and near extinction a century ago.

The snowy and great egrets, the two most persecuted egrets, have made a comeback and frequent coastal California salt marshes throughout the year. They both feed heavily on fish but take frogs, insects, and other prey.

The great egret is the larger bird, but the sure marks separating white egrets are bill and leg color. The **great egret** has black legs and a yellow bill. A small area in front of the eyes turns bright green briefly during nesting season. They feed alone or in small groups, mainly by still-hunting—freezing until prey appears.

Snowy egrets have black bills and a contrasting patch of yellow skin in front of the eye. Their legs are also black, but the feet are bright yellow. "Golden slippers" is a popular name for the bird. In young birds, a yellow stripe runs from the foot up the back of the legs. Snowy egrets sometimes feed in flocks. They often hunt actively, even sprinting through shallows after fish.

Great Egret

great egret

snowy egret

young

breeding

Snowy Egret

CHUNKY HERONS

The American bittern is primarily a freshwater bird, but it also winters in brackish coastal marshes. A bulky brown wader, it is seldom seen, but in flight, the dark trailing edge to the wing distinguishes it from young black-crowneds.

he black-crowned night-heron and green heron are bulky birds that often sit hunched up. They are differently shaped than the slender, elegant herons and egrets shown on the preceding pages. And they both feed at night to varying degrees.

The green heron, smallest of the herons, is usually seen singly at the edge of still or slow-moving water. It often crouches quietly on limbs or vegetation closely overhanging the water's surface, waiting for small fish. No heron waits more patiently. The upperparts of the **green heron** are actually blue-green. At a distance or in poor light, the bird often looks dark overall except for its bright yellow or orange legs. It gives a loud *kowp!* when disturbed.

Flocks of night-herons roost in trees when not hunting, often in daytime. They hunt singly or in small groups, usually at dusk or even at night. The black-crowned takes almost any animal it can capture and is adept at catching most, including fish.

The shape and plumage of the adult **black-crowned night-heron** are equally distinctive. Young birds go through several brown variations before achieving adult plumage in their third year. The brown young can be confused with the American bittern (see sidebar).

92

green heron

Green Heron

young

black-crowned
night-heron

**Black-crowned
Night-heron**

2nd year

young

JULIAN

SORA

VIRGINIA RAIL

Clapper rails are found year-round in a few California salt marshes. They are a larger, heavier-billed version of the Virginia rail. Their call is their best "mark," a series of percussive notes (*kek-kek-kek-kek-kek-kek*, like a wooden clapper) that start loud and then soften while accelerating.

ails are shy birds that typically remain hidden in heavy marsh vegetation. High tides sometimes force them from cover. On their freshwater nesting marshes, the sora and Virginia rail can be identified by their calls, but they call less frequently on their coastal wintering marshes. They are seen occasionally in brief flight over a marsh, although rails usually run or dive underwater when disturbed. Walking is their preferred way of getting around; with their long toes, they can walk on floating vegetation. Rails also swim, and the sora does so often.

The sora is the most numerous rail. It is primarily seen in coastal marshes in migration and winter—if seen at all. Soras eat mostly seeds. Virginia rails feed heavily on insects and other small animal prey.

The **sora** is a chunky little gray-brown waterbird. Its best marks are the short, chicken-like bill and greenish legs and toes. Adults have a black mask.

Virginia rails often share marshes with soras. They look plump from the side but are very thin, making it easy to navigate through marsh tangles. The long, reddish bill and legs and the black-and-white flanks are good marks for the **Virginia rail.** Its reddish wing patches are distinctive in flight.

young

Sora

sora

young

Virginia Rail

chick

STILT

AVOCET

oth the **stilt** and the **avocet** are striking birds that need little description beyond their illustrations. Note that the female stilt has a browner back than the male and that avocets lose their rusty heads and necks in winter. When either bird is wading, the extreme length of its legs may be concealed, but in flight, the legs trail far beyond the tail.

Much of their unique appearance results from their feeding specialties. Avocets typically wade through tide pools or other shallow impoundments, sweeping their bills side to side through the bottom sediment. They capture and eat the tiny organisms they stir up. Because the prey is small and hidden in muddy water, the avocet's bill is thin and the tips very sensitive. The upturn in the bill makes it easier to scrape the bottom sediment. Note that the female's bill is shorter and more sharply angled. When water is too deep for wading, avocets swim. They also pick small prey from exposed muddy tide flats.

Stilts can swim too, but they seldom do so. They usually pick insects or other tiny prey from the surface of still water. Their legs are so long that, on dry land, they can't pick from the ground without crouching. Stilts are fairly numerous in California's coastal marshes and salt pans.

Stilt

♂

♀

♂ summer

Avocet

♀ winter

GODWIT AND OYSTERCATCHER

MARBLED GODWIT

BLACK OYSTERCATCHER

The **marbled godwit** is a jumbo-sized sandpiper. It has an extraordinarily long bill, pink at the base, black at the tip. Since there aren't many sandpipers as large, identification is not difficult. The whimbrel and long-billed curlew in the next illustration have down-curved, not upturned, bills. The smaller dowitchers (p. 104) have long, straight bills. In flight, note the cinnamon wing linings.

Godwits are fairly numerous in loose flocks at bays, mudflats, beaches, and marshes along much of the Pacific coast in winter and during migration.

Like the stilt and avocet on the preceding illustration, the **black oystercatcher** is a "can't miss" identification. The long red bill, blackish body, and pink legs are an unmistakable combination. Young black oystercatchers are browner and their bills have dusky tips.

Oystercatchers are fairly numerous along rocky portions of the Pacific coast. Pairs or small noisy flocks feed on shellfish exposed at low tide in the intertidal zone. Their long, blade-like bills slice the muscle that clamps the shellfish shut. At high tide, oystercatchers loaf on rocks above the intertidal zone, waiting until the tide once again exposes the shellfish for feeding.

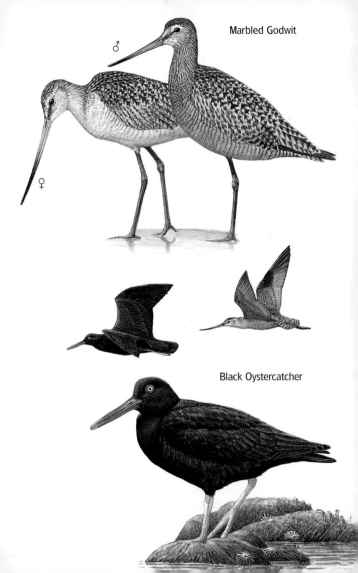

Marbled Godwit

♂

♀

Black Oystercatcher

WHIMBREL AND CURLEW

WHIMBREL

LONG-BILLED CURLEW

Although called curlews, whimbrels, and a half-dozen other names, the shorebirds in the illustrations that follow are all sandpipers, except for the plovers (pp. 110-112). Sandpipers vary in size from the long-billed curlew (23") to the least sandpiper (6").

Their size and long, down-curved bills distinguish **whimbrels** and **long-billed curlews** from other shorebirds. The same features can be used to separate them from each other. If in doubt, check the head for dark stripes; only the whimbrel has them. In flight, the bright cinnamon underwings of the long-billed curlew are a good mark.

Whimbrels and curlews are seen on the Pacific coast in winter and during migration. On the Oregon and Washington coasts, they are primarily migrants, and the long-billed is much scarcer than the whimbrel. Both are fairly numerous on the coast of California throughout the winter.

The long-billed curlew is the largest sandpiper. Females are slightly larger than males and have longer bills. The bills of young males are about the size of a whimbrel's. With its long bill, the curlew feeds at many levels in the intertidal zone.

Whimbrels feed on beaches and in the intertidal zone at low tide, especially on mudflats. Crabs are a favorite food, and the whimbrel's curved bill is the perfect shape for probing into fiddler crab burrows. Usually found in small groups, whimbrels sometimes gather in large flocks during migration.

Whimbrel

Long-billed Curlew

young ♂

YELLOWLEGS AND WILLET

LESSER YELLOWLEGS

GREATER YELLOWLEGS

WILLET

The solitary sandpiper is much like the lesser yellowlegs (including the bobbing motion) but is smaller, with a dark rump and legs. It is scarce on the coast but visits brackish marshes in migration.

The greater yellowlegs and willet are the more numerous birds. The lesser yellowlegs is scarce even on the southern California coasts where a few winter.

Seen standing, a **willet** is a big, nondescript, gray-brown sandpiper with pale blue-gray legs and bill. When flushed, it reveals the dramatic white wing stripes that are its best mark. Willets are usually seen singly or in widely spaced groups except in migration. They forage on beaches, marshes, and other coastal habitats, taking prey as large as crabs. They sometimes swim in tidal pools or deep marsh.

Bright yellow legs distinguish the yellowlegs from other coastal sandpipers. Bill length and calls are the best marks separating the **greater yellowlegs** from the **lesser.** The greater's bill is half again its head length and slightly upturned; the lesser's is about the length of its head and perfectly straight. Greater yellowlegs give a ringing flight call of three to five notes; the lesser's call is flatter and usually only one- or two-noted.

Both yellowlegs feed actively, often bobbing their heads or tails. They don't probe with their bills, but pick minnows, bugs, and other small prey from near the water's surface or at the edges of coastal marshes and tide pools.

willet

Lesser
Yellowlegs

yellowlegs (lesser)

summer

winter

Greater
Yellowlegs

summer

winter

Willet

KNOT AND DOWITCHERS

RED KNOT

SHORT-BILLED DOWITCHER

LONG-BILLED DOWITCHER

Long-billed dowitchers are illustrated. Short-bills are nearly identical, except the young have mottled tertials (the long feathers covering the folded wing), not plain. Dowitchers in summer also have mottled tertials.

Knots and dowitchers are chunky sandpipers like those in the two following illustrations. Their shapes help distinguish them from longer-necked, more slender sandpipers.

Flocks of knots migrate along the coast in spring and fall. Long-distance migrants, most winter in South America and nest in the Arctic. Some remain on the mudflats and beaches of California in winter.

In spring, their robin-red breasts distinguish **red knots** from all except the dowitchers, which have longer bills. In winter, their size and pale plumage distinguish them from everything except the dowitchers and black-bellied plovers (p. 110), all of which have distinctive bill, tail, and rump patterns.

Dowitchers are fairly numerous in the West, especially the long-billed. They feed openly in flocks in tidal pools and mudflats using a rapid vertical "stitching" motion. Snipe, the only similar long-billed bird (p. 106), are usually solitary and wary, not normally found on tidal mudflats.

Long-billed and **short-billed dowitchers** are nearly identical, and they sometimes feed in mixed flocks. Bill length is not a reliable mark separating them; flight calls are. Short-bills give a mellow *tu-tu-tu.* Long-bills give a thin, high-pitched *keek.*

Red Knot

winter

young

summer

knot

dowitcher

Dowitchers

winter

young
long-billed

summer
long-billed

SNIPE

ROCK SANDPIPER

RUDDY TURNSTONE

The snipe's wariness helped it survive the hunting pressures of the 1800s that doomed or diminished many other shorebirds.

Like the dowitchers shown on the preceding page, snipes have long bills. However, a **snipe's** plumage is darker than a dowitcher's, and snipe usually feed secretively and singly at marsh edges rather than openly in flocks on mudflats. When alarmed, they take off in rapid zigzag flight, giving a harsh *scaip* call.

The rock sandpiper and ruddy turnstone are at home on rocky shores in winter, inspecting seaweed and rock crevices for insects or other small life. Turnstones also frequent beaches and mudflats, where they often use their stubby, slightly upturned bills to probe and pry in the beach wrack.

Rock sandpipers are drab, gray-brown birds in winter, when they are found along the coast in small numbers. They are usually in small flocks of other "rock-pipers." Note the thin, slightly drooped bill. The base of the bill is greenish yellow and so are the legs.

Ruddy turnstones are fairly numerous, usually in small groups. There is nothing subtle about their summer plumage. In winter, they closely resemble the black turnstone (p. 108), having the same short, pointed bill and displaying the same harlequin back pattern in flight. The ruddy turnstone has orange legs.

snipe

Snipe

rock sandpiper
winter

winter

summer

Rock Sandpiper

turnstone
winter

summer

winter

Ruddy Turnstone

WANDERING
TATTLER

SURFBIRD

BLACK
TURNSTONE

Mixed-species flocks
of "rock-pipers" are
common in winter
and fall migration.

Wandering tattlers, surfbirds, and black turnstones feed on rocky shores like the ruddy turnstone and rock sandpiper (p. 106). The winter plumages of all five "rock-pipers" are shades of gray-brown. All except the rock sandpiper are fairly numerous in winter and during migration.

The **wandering tattler** is an even slate gray above, more uniform than the other rock-pipers. The difference is especially noticeable in flight. The best mark for standing birds is the relatively long, straight, dark bill. Tattlers are usually seen singly or in small, loose groups, and they often bob a bit while walking.

Surfbirds are usually in small groups, often with other rock-pipers, but migrating flocks can be large. In flight, the pattern of white (wing stripe, rump, and base of tail) is a sure mark for **surfbirds.** Standing birds in winter have plumages similar to the rock sandpiper's, but surfbirds are larger, with short, stout bills.

Turnstones can be distinguished from other rock-pipers by their short, pointed bills and their harlequin back pattern seen in flight. **Black turnstones** in winter lack the bib pattern of the ruddy turnstone and have dusky (not bright orange) legs. Black turnstones occasionally feed on mudflats, as well as on rocks.

summer

winter

tattler

Wandering Tattler

surfbird

winter

Surfbird

summer

turnstone

winter

Black Turnstone

summer

winter

summer

PLOVERS

AMERICAN
GOLDEN-PLOVER

BLACK-BELLIED
PLOVER

A few Pacific golden-plovers migrate along the coast and winter in coastal California.

Pacific golden-plovers in winter plumage are much like American golden-plovers, only slightly brighter yellow above. In spring, the white stripe of the Pacific golden-plover extends down its side.

Plovers are different from sandpipers. They have distinctive short, pigeon-like bills, slightly swollen at the tip. Most feed on mudflats and beaches in a characteristic stop-and-go fashion. They run a short way, pause to pick at food, then look about and scamper off again. They don't probe into the ground as sandpipers do, but pick from the surface.

The American golden-plover is seen only in fall migration on the Pacific coast, and it is scarce then. The birds begin molting out of their distinctive summer plumage during migration. Winter adult **American golden-plovers** are nearly identical to young birds. The young show some yellow mottling on their upper-parts that is lacking in the gray-brown adults. Winter golden-plovers have a darker crown and bolder eyebrow than the larger black-bellied plover and lack the black wing pits.

Black-bellied plovers are often seen on beaches and mudflats in winter and during migration. They typically forage alone, often among other smaller shorebirds, but they roost and migrate in flocks. The winter plumage is pale, with the dark eyes, bill, and legs providing sharp contrast. The striking black-and-white summer plumage is seen in spring migration. The best mark year-round is the black wing pit seen in flight.

110

summer

young

American Golden-plover

black-bellied plover

golden-plover

Black-bellied Plover

summer

winter

young

PLOVERS

KILLDEER

SNOWY PLOVER

SEMIPALMATED PLOVER

Most sandpipers don't wander from wetlands because they require sand or soft ground for probing. Plovers can pick from dry ground and wander farther from water.

Killdeer are plovers, about the size of the plovers shown on the preceding page. The two black neck bands are sure marks for the **killdeer.** In flight, the orange back and rump are obvious. Along the coast, killdeer are most often on dry (or drying) flats.

Snowy plovers are scarce and declining. They are disappearing because the sandy beaches that they use for feeding and nesting are the same ones that people use for recreation.

The dry sand above the high water line is the snowy plover's favored habitat, although they often feed at the edge of the surf. They are usually in small groups except when nesting. Their pale backs blend into a dry-sand background so well that **snowy plovers** are hard to locate even when nearby. Note the thin black bill, dusky legs, and incomplete collar.

The **semipalmated plover** is darker than the snowy and is more often seen on wet sand or mudflats. In winter plumage, it closely resembles the snowy. The best marks, besides the wet-sand back color, are the orange legs, the breast band (usually complete), and the shorter, heavier bill. The semipalmated is fairly numerous in flocks in winter and during migration. It is much more numerous than the snowy because it nests in the remote Arctic.

112

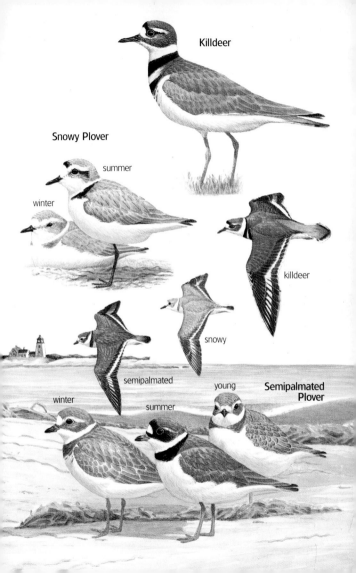

Killdeer

Snowy Plover

summer

winter

killdeer

snowy

semipalmated

winter

summer

young

Semipalmated
Plover

PHALAROPES

WILSON'S PHALAROPE

RED-NECKED PHALAROPE

Phalaropes often swim in shallow coastal marshes and tide pools. They stir up the bottom by spinning in tight circles and then pick the tiny animals that have been stirred up.

In fall, virtually all shorebirds migrate in waves. The young of the year migrate last, by themselves. Unsuccessful breeders usually migrate first.

Phalaropes, generally scarce on the coast, are usually in marshes. Wilson's phalarope appears only in migration. Fall migration actually starts in mid-June. By early October, all birds have left the US. Wilson's migrates first from its interior nesting grounds to staging areas (mostly lakes) where huge numbers can gather in preparation for the flight to wintering grounds in South America.

Females migrate first, leaving the raising of the young to the males. Males migrate after the young have fledged, and the young migrate last. Male phalaropes not only care for the young but are part of a total sex-reversal system in which the female is larger, has brighter plumage, and aggressively competes for the submissive male.

The best marks for **Wilson's phalarope** is the long, thin bill and its behavior (see sidebar). Adults are often molting from summer to winter plumage during fall migration. In flight, the white rump is a helpful mark.

Red-necked phalaropes migrate on the coast and winter at sea south of the US. Summer plumage is distinctive, but in fall, note the **red-necked phalarope's** dark "phalarope patch" through the eye; sandpipers don't have it. Also, the thin bill is shorter than Wilson's.

summer ♀ summer ♂ **Wilson's Phalarope**

winter

young

Wilson's

red-necked

young summer ♂ summer ♀ **Red-necked Phalarope**

winter

SANDPIPERS

DUNLIN

SPOTTED
SANDPIPER

The pectoral sandpiper is rare in migration along the Pacific coast, often occurring singly among other small shorebirds. It is dark brown and suggests a larger version of the least sandpiper (p. 118). The pectoral sandpiper's best mark is the way its breast streaks end sharply in a line at the belly.

The spotted sandpiper is seldom seen on open beaches or mudflats. It is more common at the water's edge on marshes, bays, and sometimes rocky shores. It walks alone (rarely with others), foraging for any small prey it can find.

The first mark noticed in a **spotted sandpiper** is that it teeters when it walks. The spotted breast is a sure plumage mark in summer; in winter, note the white wedge between the dark wing and the dark side of the breast. Flight is distinctive as well, typically over short distances and close to the water. The bird glides on bowed, quivering wings interrupted with brief series of shallow, stiff wing beats.

In migration and winter, dunlin are numerous along the coast from Canada to Mexico. They typically flock on beaches and mudflats in the intertidal zone, often with other sandpipers.

In spring, **dunlin** are bright reddish above and sport unmistakable black belly patches. A good winter (and year-round) mark is the drooped bill, longer than in most birds its size. Some western sandpipers (p. 118) have bills nearly as long, but they don't have a gray wash on their breasts in winter like dunlin. In fall, some young birds might be seen still molting into dull winter plumage.

molting young

winter

summer

Dunlin

dunlin

spotted sandpiper

summer

Spotted Sandpiper

winter

LEAST
SANDPIPER

WESTERN
SANDPIPER

SANDERLING

A few young Baird's
sandpipers are seen
in migration on the
Pacific coast in fall.
Slimmer than sander-
lings, they have breast
streaks like the least
sandpiper's. Their best
mark is long wings
extending beyond the
tail on standing birds.

The sandpipers in this illustration are the little ones commonly seen on coastal beaches and mudflats in winter and during migration. To sort them out, start with the sanderling. Any flock of sandpipers chasing the surf on a sandy beach likely are sanderlings.

In fall and winter, the **sanderling** is the palest of the small sandpipers; its black bill and legs offer noticeable contrast. Young birds (Aug.-Sept.) have black-spotted backs. In May, the upperparts, head, and breast become rusty brown, and black spots show on the back. In flight, note the broad white wing stripe.

Western and least sandpipers flock on muddy shores, marshes, and tidal flats more often than on sandy beaches. The **least sandpiper** is the smallest sandpiper in the world. It is the darkest brown of the three in winter, especial-ly on the breast. The yellow legs are a good mark year-round, but they can be darkened by mud. Also note the small, thin bill.

Western sandpipers are abundant spring and fall migrants and are numerous in California in winter. In spring, the **western sandpiper** has reddish marks on its face, head, and shoulder. Its breast streaks extend well down the sides. In fall, adults are dull gray—darker than the sanderling but lighter than the least sandpiper.

118

sanderling

least

Least Sandpiper

young

winter

summer

western

winter

summer

Western Sandpiper

young

winter

summer

Sanderling

Belted Kingfisher

♂   ♀

KINGFISHER

BELTED KINGFISHER

There is one waterbird that feeds like no other, the kingfisher. It plunge-dives for fish like some aerialists, but it doesn't glide over water searching for them. It waits on a perch beside still or slow-moving water for fish to appear. Kingfishers often hover before plunging for prey.

As one would expect because of its unique foraging style, the **belted kingfisher** looks quite different than other waterbirds. Note the large head and bill and the thick crest. Females have a rusty breast band lacking in males. Kingfishers are noisy and conspicuous. They are fairly numerous year-round along the Pacific coast wherever there are marshes or estuaries.

120

INDEX AND CHECK-LIST

How many species of birds have you identified? Keeping a record is the only way to know. Sooner or later, even the most casual bird-watcher makes notes of the species seen on a trip or in a day. People keep backyard lists, year lists, state lists, every kind of checklist. All serious birders maintain a life list. Seeing your life list grow can become part of the pleasure of bird-watching. The pages that follow are designed to serve as your checklist of coastal waterbirds as well as an index to their illustrations in this guide.

English names used in this guide and listed in the index are the familiar names used in common conversation. For the most part, they are the same as the formal English names adopted by the American Ornithologists' Union in the seventh edition of their *Check-list of North American Birds,* 1998. When the formal AOU English name differs from the common name used in this guide, the AOU English name is given on the second line of the index entry.

The Latin names in italics are the AOU's scientific names.

✓ Species		Date	Location

			Date	Location
◯	RHINOCEROS **A**UKLET *Cerorhinca monocerata*	66		
◯	**A**VOCET American Avocet *Recurvirostra americana*	96		
◯	**B**RANT *Branta bernicla*	58		
◯	**B**UFFLEHEAD *Bucephala albeola*	78		
◯	**C**ANVASBACK *Aythya valisineria*	76		
◯	**C**OOT American Coot *Fulica americana*	84		
◯	BRANDT'S **C**ORMORANT *Phalacrocorax penicillatus*	62		
◯	DOUBLE–CRESTED **C**ORMORANT *Phalacrocorax auritus*	62		
◯	PELAGIC **C**ORMORANT *Phalacrocorax pelagicus*	62		
◯	LONG–BILLED **C**URLEW *Numenius americanus*	100		
◯	LONG–BILLED **D**OWITCHER *Limnodromus scolopaceus*	104		
◯	SHORT–BILLED **D**OWITCHER *Limnodromus griseus*	104		
◯	HARLEQUIN **D**UCK *Histrionicus histrionicus*	78		
◯	RING–NECKED **D**UCK *Aythya collaris*	74		
◯	RUDDY **D**UCK *Oxyura jamaicensis*	76		
◯	**D**UNLIN *Calidris alpina*	116		

✓ Species	Date	Location

○ **GREAT EGRET** 90
Ardea alba

○ **SNOWY EGRET** 90
Egretta thula

○ **FULMAR** 34
Northern Fulmar
Fulmarus glacialis

○ **GADWALL** 70
Anas strepera

○ **MARBLED GODWIT** 98
Limosa fedoa

○ **AMERICAN GOLDEN-PLOVER** 110
Pluvialis dominica

○ **BARROW'S GOLDENEYE** 80
Bucephala islandica

○ **COMMON GOLDENEYE** 80
Bucephala clangula

○ **CANADA GOOSE** 58
Branta canadensis

○ **SNOW GOOSE** 56
Chen caerulescens

○ **WHITE-FRONTED GOOSE** 56
Greater White-fronted Goose
Anser albifrons

○ **CLARK'S GREBE** 84
Aechmophorus clarkii

○ **EARED GREBE** 86
Podiceps nigricollis

○ **HORNED GREBE** 86
Podiceps auritus

○ **RED-NECKED GREBE** 86
Podiceps grisegena

○ **WESTERN GREBE** 84
Aechmophorus occidentalis

✓ Species	Date	Location

○ PIGEON **G**UILLEMOT 64
Cepphus columba

○ BONAPARTE'S **G**ULL 44
Larus philadelphia

○ CALIFORNIA **G**ULL 40
Larus californicus

○ GLAUCOUS-WINGED **G**ULL 38
Larus glaucescens

○ HEERMANN'S **G**ULL 44
Larus heermanni

○ HERRING **G**ULL 40
Larus argentatus

○ MEW **G**ULL 42
Larus canus

○ RING-BILLED **G**ULL 42
Larus delawarensis

○ WESTERN **G**ULL 38
Larus occidentalis

○ GREAT BLUE **H**ERON 88
Ardea herodias

○ GREEN **H**ERON 92
Butorides virescens

○ PARASITIC **J**AEGER 32
Stercorarius parasiticus

○ **K**ILLDEER 112
Charadrius vociferus

○ BELTED **K**INGFISHER 120
Ceryle alcyon

○ BLACK-LEGGED **K**ITTIWAKE 32
Rissa tridactyla

○ RED **K**NOT 104
Calidris canutus

○ COMMON **L**OON 60
Gavia immer

✓ Species	Date	Location

○ PACIFIC **L**OON 60
  Gavia pacifica

○ RED–THROATED **L**OON 60
  Gavia stellata

○ **M**ALLARD 68
  Anas platyrhynchos

○ RED–BREASTED **M**ERGANSER 84
  Mergus serrator

○ COMMON **M**URRE 64
  Uria aalge

○ MARBLED **M**URRELET 66
  Brachyramphus marmoratus

○ BLACK-CROWNED **N**IGHT-HERON 92
  Nycticorax nycticorax

○ BLACK **O**YSTERCATCHER 98
  Haematopus bachmani

○ BROWN **P**ELICAN 36
  Pelecanus occidentalis

○ WHITE **P**ELICAN 54
  American White Pelican
  Pelecanus erythrorhynchos

○ RED–NECKED **P**HALAROPE 114
  Phalaropus lobatus

○ WILSON'S **P**HALAROPE 114
  Phalaropus tricolor

○ **P**INTAIL 70
  Northern Pintail
  Anas acuta

○ BLACK–BELLIED **P**LOVER 110
  Pluvialis squatarola

○ SNOWY **P**LOVER 112
  Charadrius alexandrinus

○ SEMIPALMATED **P**LOVER 112
  Charadrius semipalmatus

✓ Species	Date	Location
◯ VIRGINIA **R**AIL *Rallus limicola*	94	
◯ **R**EDHEAD *Aythya americana*	76	
◯ **S**ANDERLING *Calidris alba*	118	
◯ LEAST **S**ANDPIPER *Calidris minutilla*	118	
◯ ROCK **S**ANDPIPER *Calidris ptilocnemis*	106	
◯ SPOTTED **S**ANDPIPER *Actitis macularia*	116	
◯ WESTERN **S**ANDPIPER *Calidris mauri*	118	
◯ GREATER **S**CAUP *Aythya marila*	74	
◯ LESSER **S**CAUP *Aythya affinis*	74	
◯ BLACK **S**COTER *Melanitta nigra*	82	
◯ SURF **S**COTER *Melanitta perspicillata*	82	
◯ WHITE−WINGED **S**COTER *Melanitta fusca*	82	
◯ BLACK-VENTED **S**HEARWATER *Puffinus opisthomelas*	34	
◯ SOOTY **S**HEARWATER *Puffinus griseus*	34	
◯ **S**HOVELER Northern Shoveler *Anas clypeata*	68	
◯ **S**NIPE Common Snipe *Gallinago gallinago*	106	

How to use our guide

- All the practical information, hints and tips that you will need before and during the trip start on page 100.
- For general background, see the sections Amsterdam and its People, p. 6, and A Brief History, p. 12.
- All the sights to see are listed between pages 26 and 61, with suggestions on daytrips and excursions from Amsterdam on pages 62 to 82. Our own choice of sights most highly recommended is pinpointed by the Berlitz traveller symbol.
- Entertainment, nightlife and all other leisure activities are described between pages 83 and 92, while information on restaurants and cuisine is to be found on pages 92 to 99.
- Finally, there is an index at the back of the book, pp. 126–128.

Found an error or an omission in this Berlitz Guide? Or a change or new feature we should know about? Our editor would be happy to hear from you, and a postcard would do. Be sure to include your name and address, since in appreciation for a useful suggestion, we'd like to send you a travel guide. Write to: Berlitz Publishing Co. Ltd., London Road, Wheatley, Oxford OX9 1YR, England.

Although we make every effort to ensure the accuracy of all the information in this book, changes occur incessantly. We cannot therefore take responsibility for facts, prices, addresses and circumstances in general that are constantly subject to alteration.

Text: Vernon Leonard
Photography: Suki Langereis, pp. 8, 9, 41 Jean Kugler; pp. 17, 29 PRISMA/Etienne; pp. 31, 57 PRISMA/Worldview; p. 45 PRISMA/Hauk; p. 52 PRISMA/Wagner; p. 55 André Held, Ecublens; p. 71 KLM Aerocarto
Layout: Doris Haldemann
We would like to thank Marianne Bielders, Anne Bijleveld, Thérèse van Gelder, Piet van der Vet and Carolyn Thornton for their help in updating this guide.
4 Cartography: *Falk* Falk-Verlag, Hamburg.

Contents

Amsterdam and its People

Amsterdam is a contrary city. One minute it's a perfect picture postcard. The next minute there's a naughty smile on its face.

The central area is a unique 17th-century museum, often called the Venice of the North. Row upon row of gabled houses lean crazily against one another along a network of tree-lined canals. Vistas of venerable churches stretch beyond white wooden drawbridges, narrow cobbled streets and myriads of barges...

But why do Amsterdammers insist on driving at breakneck speeds through their "museum"? Do they really want to shatter all these 17th-century images?

On Sunday mornings it's a hamlet of innocence, quiet and reverential as an old religious

tapestry. Red lights here? Pre-posterous!

Then it's Monday again, and the denizens are back making money: unloading giant trucks in impossible alleys; blocking traffic with laughable disdain; dodging the hordes of cyclists, who don't seem to care much about traffic regulations.

Comes a lull in the traffic. The clear bells of the Wester-kerk break through from Amsterdam's tallest church tower, playing "John Brown's Body" or some other unlikely tune. The Mint Tower carillon chimes in, as do the bells of the Royal Palace on Dam Square. Below, amid the shopping crowds, one of the city's eight street organs grinds away.

Strand three Amsterdam-mers on a desert island, it's said, and they'll organize three

Surreal reflections on the split personality of stately Amsterdam.

political parties. They love a friendly argument, particularly if they can shock the rest of conformist Holland. They have loud discussions in bars. They parade with banners like other people change their socks. Most Dutch protests begin or end on Dam Square, Amsterdam. Even a City Hall

booklet admits it: of 700,000 Amsterdammers, 699,999 are obstinate Amsterdammers.

But then out comes that smile again, to welcome strangers. Ask them the way, and there's not a gram of resentment if you don't speak difficult Dutch. They will answer you in English, German or French, perhaps Spanish and Italian, too, and if you put up a language that beats them they'll ask the next passer-by if he can help.

Along with London, Paris and Rome, Amsterdam is one of Europe's most popular tourist cities—thanks, certainly, to the warm-hearted welcome its inhabitants extend to foreigners but, above all, to the picturesque Golden Age look of the town's central canal area.

Essentially, this is a lived-in museum of a city centre. It does not empty at 6 p.m.: the trucks will disappear, but many workers will drive from modern offices and factories in the suburbs back to their homes in the centre.

They'll be back amid their local shops, in village-like

Central Station offers a grandiose welcome to Amsterdam.

streets between the canals, where there's still a friendly butcher, baker and grocer.

And this is the way City Hall likes it. The Golden Age character is preserved by statute. At last count, 7,000 buildings were classified as protected monuments. Complete 17th-century residential areas are renovated, rather than replaced with office blocks. However, of late, Amsterdam has been developing ambitious plans for hotels, offices and luxury apartments in the city centre and on the riverbanks.

Amsterdam is a remarkable mixture: a capital without a government (the latter is 40 minutes down the road in The Hague); a city of canals and houseboats where the bicycle, however, is king; a mecca of art, where the Rijksmuseum and the Van Gogh collection vie with the red-light district as prime tourist attractions; prim plant-filled suburban

homes contrast with city-centre sex shops and gay bars; a gourmet's delight, with anything from traditional raw herring to an Indonesian *rijsttafel* on the menu.

More than 100 nationalities live together, on the whole harmoniously, in this flourishing 17th-century port-town.

The face of the city, however, is not without its scars, albeit they seem nowadays to be less and less visible. The housing shortage that once plagued the city and created an army of squatters has abated. And the drug dilemma, with its attendant violence, appears somewhat stabilized. But these are problems familiar to most of the world's large cities. Amsterdam is taking it all in its stride and trying to find solutions, reasonable and equitable, as it always has.

Perky Lieverdje *statue (left) ; Mokum scrawl is Amsterdam's nickname. Below, elegant Herengracht.*

A Brief History

The Batavians floated down the Rhine in hollowed-out tree trunks. At least, that's how legend evocatively depicts the arrival of the first settlers in these parts.

Be that as it may, the Romans, who came here more to trade than to conquer, record the presence of this and related tribes, including the Frisians, by the sea shortly before the birth of Christ. Lat-

er, the Franks, Saxons and other Germanic tribes expanded into the area during the massive migrations of the Germanic peoples in the 5th century which heralded the beginning of the Dark Ages. Christianity, which had established a tenuous hold under Roman influence, was van-

A view of Amsterdam in 1538 shows the heart of today's city.

quished; despite the efforts of a handful of courageous missionaries, it was more than 300 years after the demise of Roman power before the pagan tribes were converted.

Until well into the Middle Ages, the descendants of these peoples scarcely impinged upon the great events which were slowly but surely forging a new Europe out of the chaos that reigned at the fall of the Roman empire. Charlemagne and his empire came and went, and the Netherlands remained an amalgam of small states ruled by counts, dukes and bishops.

One group, probably the Waterlanders from the region just north of the IJ*, moved to slightly less waterlogged ground and beached their boats on a sandbank where the river Amstel runs into the IJ. They dammed the river to prevent the tides from sweeping in. As a consequence of the dam, cargoes had to be transshipped between sea-going and river vessels, providing an additional source of revenue for the local community. The settlement became known as Amstelredamme.

* A long broad inlet from the Zuyder Zee. (IJ, pronounced somewhere between eye and ay, is treated as a single letter in the Dutch language.)

In 1275, Count Floris V of Holland granted a toll freedom to the local citizenry, and it is from this year that Amsterdammers traditionally count the founding of their city. The dam built over 700 years ago was located exactly where Dam Square and the Royal Palace are now.

From Fishing Village to Metropolis

At first, the expansion of the Waterlanders' fishing village was hardly spectacular. But in 1345 a totally incongruous occurrence provided a turning point for the community's fortunes. A piece of communion bread a sick man had tried unsuccessfully to swallow failed to burn in the fireplace. The event was declared a miracle, and Amsterdam became a place of pilgrimage for Christians of the Middle Ages.

And thereafter, commerce thrived. An increasing number of ships used the port, and they came from further afield: from the Baltic, from France, from England, sailing in past the northern island of Texel and down the shallow Zuyder Zee to a safe anchorage at sheltered Amsterdam.

A century later, in 1452, fire almost destroyed the wooden 13 town, and from then it became compulsory to build with bricks. Colourful gables also replaced the old wooden signs denoting trades, professions and names, and the town took on a permanent look.

By the beginning of the 16th century, Amsterdam counted 2,000 houses and a vast number of monasteries and convents, with 15,000 inhabitants. During the next 50 years the town almost trebled in size. The most significant factor in the rapid 16th-century growth was the general spirit of revolt against Spanish domination. While most of the Low Countries laboured under harsh foreign rule, Amsterdam was neutral for a long time, attracting large numbers of often talented refugees (such as the diamond-cutters from Spanish-devastated Antwerp).

Under the Spanish Yoke
After centuries of belonging to nobody but themselves, most of the Low Countries (the present-day Netherlands and Belgium) had, in the early 15th century, fallen under the sway of the Burgundians, a once-powerful state whose Dukes' bequest to posterity has been the name of a celebrated wine-producing region in France. In 1506, as a result of a series of treaties and intrigues, marriages and deaths, these territories became part of the heritage that eventually established Charles, Duke of Burgundy (a Hapsburg) as Holy Roman Emperor and King of Spain, ruler of a realm on which "the sun never set".

Though Charles V was born in Flanders, Spain was the heart of his empire. He proved less than sympathetic to his subjects back in the Netherlands, whose growing wealth made them a target for heavy imperial taxation. Above all, Charles fiercely opposed the challenge to the Catholic church, the papacy and Catholic rulers such as himself, presented by the Reformation. The Reformation had spread outwards from Germany to become firmly rooted in the northern, Dutch, areas of Spain's Netherlands province, and in an attempt to burn out the infection, Charles introduced the Inquisition there in the 1520s.

Charles' successor, his son Philip II of Spain, pursued his father's anti-Reformation policy with the utmost vigour. In 1567 he sent the ruthless Duke of Alva to the Netherlands to settle the religious issue and establish a military dictatorship.

Struggle for Independence

An era of terror and torture began—a period of warfare which was to last 80 years. Out of the resistance emerged the liberal thinker and spirited leader of the Dutch rebels, Prince William (dubbed the Silent) of the House of Orange*, founder of the dynasty which has reigned as *stadhouder* (governor) or monarch over the Netherlands practically ever since. His

Van der Velde's Burning of the English Fleet at Chatham *highlights 17th-century supremacy.*

cause continued to gather momentum, particularly after the brutal 1572 massacre of the Protestant Huguenots in France.

While violence raged all over the country and many towns—including Alkmaar, Haarlem and Leiden—suffered the hardships of battle, siege or occupation, Amsterdam remained loyal to the King of Spain. It wasn't until 1578 that this important trading city, already renowned for its religious tolerance (it had **15**

---

* William's forbears originally came from the former minor principality of Orange, just north of Avignon in the Rhône valley. He himself had inherited extensive estates in the Netherlands, hence his involvement in the struggle.

taken in Portuguese Jews fleeing from the Inquisition, Protestant Huguenots who had been persecuted in France and English dissenters), finally declared for the cause of freedom from Spanish rule.

In 1579, the seven largely Protestant provinces north of the Rhine (called the United Provinces) concluded the Treaty of Utrecht, and before long this break between the northern and the southern provinces became permanent. In the south (where many of the people were French-speaking Walloons) even Catholics had joined in the resistance to the cruel tyranny of the Spaniards. However, the Spanish army had managed to maintain its hold on these areas, and the long-term consequence of the ensuing north-south split was the separate existence of today's Netherlands and Belgium. Meanwhile, before he was murdered in 1584, William had become the founding father of Dutch independence—at the same time that Elizabeth's England was also defying the Spain of Philip II. The struggle was brilliantly pursued by William's sons, Maurice and Frederick Henry.

More territory was subsequently gained in the south and south-east, and when the treaties of The Hague and of Westphalia were signed in 1648 (marking the end of the Thirty Years' War in Europe), the independent state of the Netherlands, practically as it looks today, was internationally recognized.

The Golden Age
But even before the Netherlands had gained their freedom from Spain, the Dutch Golden Age had begun to burgeon. In the early 16th century, the Dutch had already provided northern Europe with its greatest representative of the Renaissance—Erasmus. The combined skills of the merchant class, scientists, artists and craftsmen, both native and imported, now created a climate so fertile that one enterprise followed another and turned the 17th century into that of Holland's glory.

By the end of the 15th century, the Portuguese had pioneered the sea route to the East Indies, and Lisbon became an emporium for Indian products. Not content with Baltic trade, Dutch merchants began buying these up and shipping them to northern Europe where they were sold at considerable profit. It was only a short step (provoked by

Spain's conquest of Portugal) to extend their voyages and fetch the merchandise themselves from the Far East. As competition grew and profits fell, Amsterdam's shipowners decided to form a single company, the Dutch East Indies Company (*Verenigde Oostindische Compagnie*, or *VOC*), which was granted a monopoly for trade with all countries east of the Cape of Good Hope. It soon became one of the most powerful commercial organizations the world had ever known. At its height, the VOC owned 150 merchant ships, 40 warships and 10,000 soldiers. Under its flag sailed some of Holland's greatest sea heroes. It paid a dividend of 40 per cent, and Amsterdam was its most influential and biggest shareholder.

The VOC's major foreign base was Batavia (now Jakarta) on Java, but from Amsterdam Henry Hudson was also sent in search of a new route to China. Instead, in 1609, he discovered the river that bears his name, and New Amsterdam, forerunner of New York, was founded as a Dutch town on the island of Manhattan, then unknown.

Dutch sailors of the VOC were the first white men to land in Australia, 150 years before Captain Cook. Abel Tasman charted much of its coastline and discovered Tasmania, New Zealand and the Fiji Islands.

The Dutch Father Christmas lands once a year at St. Nicholas' Church on the harbourfront.

Jan van Riebeeck created a victualling and medical station at Cape Town, the halfway point on the Dutch route to the East. Ceylon was colonized, as were parts of Brazil and the Caribbean. Off Nagasaki, the Dutch trading post was the only one allowed to deal with Japan during the 200 years of the Shogun isolation.

If the Far Eastern trade was more exotic, and extremely profitable, European commerce remained even more important. Goods from as far afield as the White Sea and Baltic ports and Mediterranean countries were brought to Amsterdam by Dutch merchantmen and sold throughout western Europe. Even English and French coastal trade was largely in Dutch hands.

The Fruits of Enterprise
All this brought tremendous wealth to the Netherlands (whose population was little more than 1 million) and most of all to Amsterdam, which held 50 per cent of all Dutch trade in its hands.

Amsterdam had indeed become the first port and market of the world and, with its 200,000 inhabitants, was bursting at its seams. Its original crescent of canals was extended outwards around the River Amstel, to the horse-shoe layout we see today.

As industry and commerce expanded, pinnacles were reached in the arts, particularly painting. This was the age of Rembrandt, Frans Hals, Vermeer, Jan Steen and Paulus Potter, to name but a few.

It was during this age, too, that Dutch scientists and military men gained world respect. Antonie van Leeuwenhoek invented the microscope. Herman Boerhaave's lectures in medicine attracted students from all over Europe. Prince Maurice, son of William the Silent, had developed new, sophisticated military tactics which now spread over the continent.

The rise of the United Provinces to a position of eminence as the world's foremost maritime power led to rivalry with England, which erupted in a series of wars between the two countries. In the second Anglo-Dutch war (1665-67), England was nearly brought to its knees when Holland's greatest sea hero, Admiral de Ruyter, caused panic in London by his audacious raid up the River Medway as far as Chatham to burn the English fleet and tow home in triumph the flagship *Royal Charles* (part of her stern decoration can still be seen in the Rijksmuseum).

Decline

But the dynamic energy of the 1600s began to flag; and the 18th century was a quiet period, characterized more by an aping of the French way of life than by indigenous development.

In 1776, England's rebellious North American colonies found a ready ally in the Netherlands. From the canalsides of Amsterdam, the merchants supplied them, via the Dutch Caribbean island of St. Eustatius, with much-needed supplies and ammunition, and made huge loans to set the new country on its feet.

Needless to say, such actions drew down British wrath, and the Anglo-Dutch war of 1780, in which British sea supremacy began to be felt, sounded the death knell of the once-so-powerful Dutch trading companies. Amsterdam's prosperity declined. Finally, in 1795, Napoleon's armies over-ran the United Provinces and the Golden Age was well and truly a memory.

The years of French rule saw an upturn in elegance and culture in Amsterdam, but a low point in commercial activity. Louis Bonaparte, younger brother of the emperor, was set up as King of Holland and turned the town hall on Dam Square into his palace (some of his superb furniture is still on view there—see pp. 57–58). However, in 1810 he fled the city overnight after his brother severely criticized his lax administration.

Holland now lost any semblance of independence and was annexed by France. The Dutch grew restless, and the cry *Oranje boven!* (Up with the House of Orange!) was heard again. In 1813, as Napoleon's star began to sink, the exiled Prince William of Orange was proclaimed the country's first king.

A Modern Nation Develops

With the establishment of the new monarchy, the modern Netherlands were born.

The 19th century was one of steady local progress for Amsterdam rather than the international glitter of before. The economic rot had first to be halted—and then came the simultaneous problems and advantages of the industrial revolution.

Vast new housing areas were needed, some of which soon degenerated into slums. **19**

But as the century advanced, better homes were built, along with museums and centres for learning and the performing arts.

The basis of Holland's social welfare system was laid down during this period and, in the diamond industry, workers formed a trade union that was said to be the model of modern unionism.

To revitalize Amsterdam's port, the North Holland Canal was dug from Den Helder in the north and the even more important North Sea Canal from IJmuiden on the coast.

The 20th Century

After the First World War, during which Holland remained neutral, spectacular progress was made in land reclamation in the sea: in the 1920s and 30s, the old, tidal Zuyder Zee was transformed into a freshwater lake by the construction of the 19-mile enclosing dike (Afsluitdijk), and its waters partially pumped out to create new land.

In the Second World War, Holland was not so lucky. Despite its protestations of neutrality, it was invaded by the Germans in spring, 1940. Five years of hardship followed. Despite a courageous protest

Holland and the Netherlands

To a Dutchman, the word Holland does not mean the whole country. That's the Netherlands.

North Holland (which includes Amsterdam) and South Holland (including The Hague and Rotterdam) are just two of the country's 12 provinces.

The other 10 are: Drenthe, Friesland, Gelderland, Groningen, Limburg, North Brabant, Overijssel, Utrecht, Flevoland and Zeeland.

strike mounted by Dutch dockworkers in 1941, most of Amsterdam's Jews were sent to concentration camps. The winter of 1944–45 was one of near-starvation in Amsterdam and the north after the Allied advance was halted. The valiant will of the Dutch to survive as an independent nation was bolstered by Queen Wilhelmina's defiant broadcasts from London where she had fled only after extreme diplomatic pressure.

The devastation of war, and the reduction of the Netherlands to a modest European trading nation stripped of its former East Indies colony, produced a will to work for recovery that hallmarked the postwar years. Industry grew, but at the same time protective legislation was introduced to ensure that cities like Amsterdam did not lose their architectural characteristics of bygone days.

Besides developing within their own country a highly advanced welfare system, the post-war Dutch have been firm supporters of the movement for European integration in the form of the Common Market. They've also replaced their former reliance on neutrality by membership of NATO. The economy of the Netherlands flourishes, and the Guilder is now one of the strongest of the European currencies.

Yet all this security and prosperity hasn't led to complacency. One thing is certain, if you know the Amsterdammer: restless merchant-adventurer at heart, he is not the person to stand still for very long.

Pattern of Amsterdam's canals has not changed since the Golden Age.

Gables and Gablestones

Look up at the gables in Amsterdam. Look halfway up the old buildings, also, to see the *gevelstenen* (gablestones) that date from before the French occupation of 1795.

Gablestones were a pictorial language of their own. They were sculpted, and often coloured, symbols of an owner's name, town of origin, religious belief or, more usually, his occupation.

An ox-head still adorning Nieuwendijk 406 refers back to a former owner who was a hide-dealer. A gablestone showing a man wielding a scythe at Bethaniëndwarsstraat 18 dates back to 1623.

There are city scenes and lambs, blacksmiths and grain carriers—and a yawning man in Gravenstraat, traditional sign for a druggist.

This Amsterdam address system baffled the French. It was they who first numbered the houses in each street.

Gablestones (left) were 'address plates' for rich men's houses. Merchants graced their residences with step, neck or bell gables (right) to enhance their property.

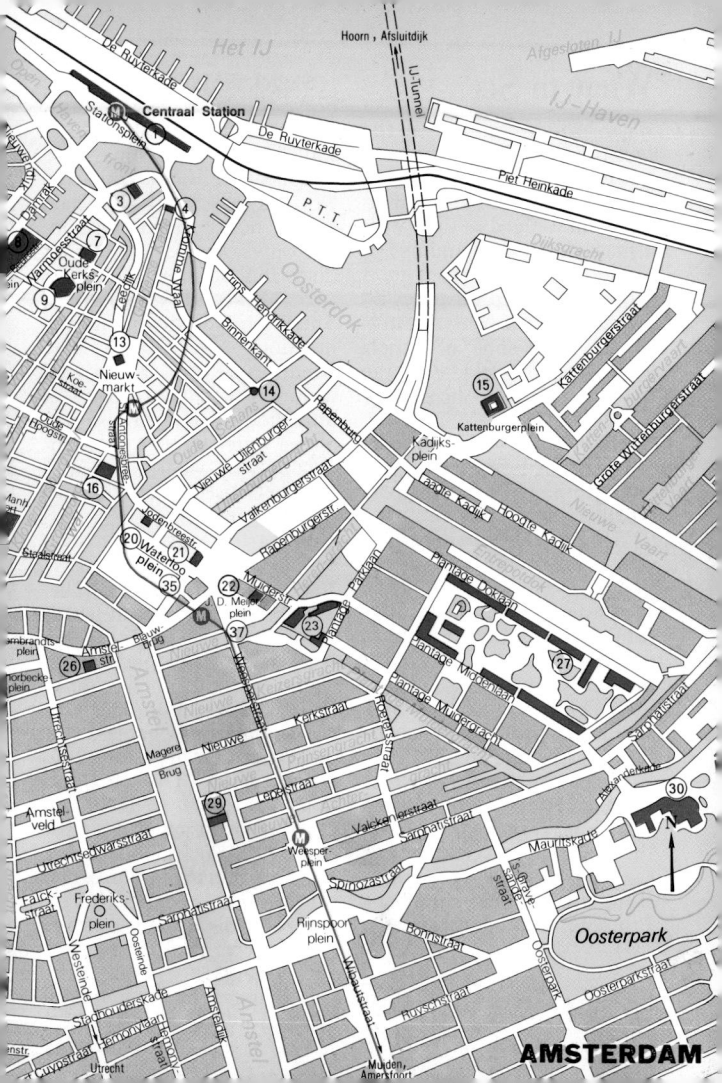

AMSTERDAM

What to See

It can look so confusing to the first-time visitor: an apparent maze of canals, all approximately the same size, all tree-lined, all wedged in tight with a mass of gabled buildings.

But pause and take a good look at our map on pages 24 and 25. Central Amsterdam is like a horse-shoe of canals split down the middle by the Damrak – Rokin – Vijzelstraat main street.

Then jump aboard the nearest tour-boat for a **canal trip** (see p. 106). It's the best introduction to the city.

While you're relaxing on the boat and listening to the multilingual tour guide, you'll see the pattern more clearly. The four main concentric canals are running parallel to each other as they swing around, linked every now and again by small cross-canals, and each has a distinctive character.

Main canal (gracht) names to memorize are: the Singel* (which means ring, or girdle), the Herengracht (Gentlemen's Canal), the Keizersgracht (Emperor's Canal), and the Prinsengracht (Princes' Canal).

---

* Not to be confused with the Singelgracht, another encircling canal further out.

Singel, the inner canal of the horse-shoe, was once the city's fortified boundary, though the wall behind it has long since disappeared. Look out for No. 7, a real oddity—the narrowest house in Amsterdam. It's only as wide as its front door and is jammed between two 17th-century buildings. Three bridges down, at the junction with Oude Leliestraat, note the iron-barred windows of a quaint old jail set into the bridge itself and just above water level. Approachable only by water, it's said to have been used to keep drunks quiet overnight.

From the Singel, the town spread outwards in the early 1600s to **Herengracht.** This was the No. 1 canal on which to live during the city's Golden Age. The wealthiest merchants vied with each other to build the widest homes, the most elaborate gables, the most impressive front entrance steps. The patrician houses are still here in all their glory, though most are now too big for private residence and are occupied by banks and offices. One exception is No. 502, official residence of the Burgomaster (Lord Mayor) of Amsterdam.

Keizersgracht was named after Holy Roman Emperor

Maximilian I, whose realm also included the Netherlands. The houses on this canal are not quite as grand as on Herengracht, but they are still charming and solid middle-class. Look out for No. 123, the "House of the Six Heads" *(Huis met de hoofden)*. You'll see the heads carved on the façade. They are said to represent six burglars who were caught while breaking in and beheaded by a maid, whose bravery was thus commemorated in stone.

Canal-tour 'buses' provide a very convenient way of sightseeing.

Prinsengracht, the last main canal of the horse-shoe, is much more down-to-earth, with smaller homes and many warehouses still in their original condition. A good number of the picturesque warehouses are officially protected from demolition, and some have now been transformed into luxury apartments—in great demand by the booming yuppie culture.

The ubiquitous Amsterdam hoisting-beam for goods is still affixed to the warehouses, but nowadays its main use is in getting the well-off tenants' new sofas upstairs.

Along all the canals is a splendid variety of façades and gables. Because most houses were built so narrow (city tax was levied in the old days according to canal frontage), the only real chance for individual embellishment was on the gable, which has become synonymous with Dutch architecture of the 17th century (see pp. 22–23). The wider homes topped by cornices and parapets are usually French-influenced 18th-century buildings, often called Louis houses.

Life afloat in a floating city— even sturdy warehouses lean tipsily on wooden piles.

Looking around from your canal-boat seat, you'll quickly gather that this is a city with more canals than Venice, more bicycles than Copenhagen, and a kaleidoscopic jumble of houseboats like nothing else on earth. The 2,500 houseboats range from luxury living to simple rafts, from a cats' home to a floating pottery. About 500 are not actually licensed to moor but, according to city plans, soon will be.

Yes, the one-hour canal tour is a must. It shows you Amsterdam in a nutshell—historic and charming, pragmatic and businesslike, and always

with a touch of liberalism that borders on the bizarre. You might also consider taking another tour in the late evening, for during the season the main canals and bridges are floodlit after dusk. You can then choose between a routine evening tour, which is similar to the day tour, or a "candle-light tour", a romantic trip with wine and snacks included in the higher price—an unforgettable experience.

Because the central part of Amsterdam is relatively compact, it's also easy to visit on foot. Women should be sure to pack low-heeled, comfortable shoes to deal with the cobbled streets. The best idea is to split the centre into four sections as we have done in the following pages, and cover one at a time.

South-West Section:
between Vondel Park and Muntplein

Leidseplein (*plein* = square) is the site of the old city gate on the road to Leiden. Today, the gate, the markets and the carriages have gone, and in their place is a multitude of restaurants and sandwich shops, outdoor cafés and cinemas, discotheques, night-clubs and bars—with several major airline offices squeezed in between. There's always a bustle of activity on Leidseplein, one of the city's focal points for tourists. In winter, an ice-hockey rink occupies the middle of the square.

The north-west side of the square is dominated by the Stadsschouwburg (Municipal Theatre), with its pillared entrance. Built in 1894, it houses the Toneelgroep Amsterdam and is host to a lot of visiting.

The American Hotel, virtually next door to the theatre, is something of a city tradition. A building full of character begun in 1880, it has a magnificent **Jugendstil restaurant**, protected by the authorities as an architectural monument. This has become a meeting place for sightseeing tourists, students and anyone who likes to chat and be seen.

Vondel Park is only 200 yards away, to the south-west. This "lung" for the densely built city centre is named after Holland's foremost poet, the 17th-century Joost van den Vondel. Its 120 acres include lawns, lakes and flower displays (see also p. 109). The park boasts the **Filmmuseum** (3 films a day) and in summer it hosts an open-air music and theatre festival.

Nearby Museumplein, a broad, grassy square wild with crocuses and daffodils in spring, is bordered by four major museums and the city's main concert hall.

Stop for a drink in Leidseplein— if you can find an empty seat.

Looking down the square from its rightful place at the top is the palace-like **Rijksmuseum,** designed by Petrus Cuypers and opened in 1885, home of one of the world's great art collections, including Rembrandt's *Night Watch.* On the right-hand side of the square, looking down from

the Rijksmuseum, are the **Vincent van Gogh Museum** designed by Gerrit Rietveld, its glass-box exterior looking something of an anachronism on the square, and the **Stedelijk Museum** (Municipal Museum) containing the city's rich collection of modern art. Nobody on a visit to Amsterdam will willingly forgo a visit to the Rijksmuseum, and all three will be on the art-lover's list of priorities. For a description of their exhibits, see MUSEUMS, pp. 53–60.

On the bottom side of the square is the Concertgebouw (Concert Hall), home of the world-famous orchestra of the same name. Opened in 1888, during a boom-time for Amsterdam cultural building, it has a main hall which seats 2,200 people and is renowned for its near-perfect acoustics.

From the bottom of Museumplein you can make your way back to Leidseplein by going north along Van Baerlestraat and turning right down P.C. Hooftstraat, the two streets which constitute Amsterdam's modest centre of haute couture. Or you might take a long detour by way of Nieuwe Spiegelstraat to inspect the numerous antique shops.

Heading north-east from Leidseplein this time, you come straight into Leidsestraat, banned to all traffic but trams. Leidsestraat was once the top shopping street in town, and you can still find some quality stores along it, amongst all the airline offices and sandwich shops.

Definitely make a point of seeing the **floating flower market** *(drijvende bloemenmarkt)* to the right at the top of Leidsestraat, along the Singel canal. Here for more than 200 years Amsterdammers have stepped aboard the gently swaying, floating shop-boats moored at the canalside to buy the profusion of plants and flowers that you'll see in the windows of their homes, all around. Plants overflow onto the canalside over a 200-yard stretch that sometimes resembles a miniature jungle.

The **Munttoren** (Mint Tower) overlooks this colourful scene, its 17th-century carillon adding an extra touch of gaiety by chiming out an old Dutch tune every half-hour. The tower was originally a medieval gate in the fortified wall of the Singel canal. Fire destroyed the upper part of the gate in 1619, and the present decorative little clock tower was added a year later by Hendrick de Keyser, town architect and best-known stone-mason of his day in Holland. In 1672, the Dutch war with France, England, Münster and Cologne temporarily cut off money supplies to Amsterdam, and the city minted its own in this building. The name has remained since then.

A few hundred yards north of the floating flower market is the **Begijnhof** (Beguine Court), a charming haven of quiet in the heart of the busy city. It's somewhat hidden behind an

The tranquil Begijnhof precinct and (below) the floating flower market vie for tourist attention.

arched oak doorway on Spui, opposite a university building. Inside is a neat quadrangle of lawn surrounded by perfect 17th- and 18th-century almshouses, two small churches and a 15th-century wooden house. English Pilgrim Fathers who fled to Holland before joining the *Mayflower* prayed regularly in the Beguine Court church dating originally from 1392 and known since 1607 as the Scottish Presbyterian Church. Opposite is the Catholic church which nuns were allowed to install in two of the almshouses during the Calvinist domination of Amsterdam in the 17th century. One of its fine stained-glass windows commemorates the "wafer miracle" of 1345 (see p. 13).

The court was originally founded in 1346 for the benefit of the Beguines, members of a Dutch lay sisterhood not bound by vows. Today, the Beguine Court's houses, each with its own tiny front garden, are occupied at a nominal rent by elderly women citizens. They are the smartest, youngest-looking old ladies you could wish to see.

Music in the air: old melodies from Mint Tower; street organs are welcome sounds of the city.

North-West Section:

between Kalverstraat and the Jordaan

Leaving the Beguine Court by the rear gate, you are straight into the vast **Amsterdams Historisch Museum** (Amsterdam Historical Museum), newly restored after serving as an or-

22 old city gablestones have been restored and set into the wall.

If you leave by the Kalverstraat exit, you can continue north in the company of the shopping crowds on this pedestrian-only street to Amsterdam's main square.

Dam Square (called simply

phanage for almost 400 years. Its many rooms and galleries tell the city's fascinating story from 1275 to 1945, with exhibits ranging from prehistoric remains and the city's original charter to audio-visual slide shows on land reclamation. Don't miss a peek at the St. Luciënsteeg entrance, where

Dam in Dutch) is the city's heart and *raison d'être,* a no-frills area always throbbing with life. It was here that the river Amstel was dammed some time before 1275, eventually to be filled in completely along Damrak and Rokin.

Dam Square is dominated by the **Koninklijk Paleis**

(Royal Palace). Opened as the Town Hall in 1655 in the prosperous Golden Age, it was converted into a palace by Louis Bonaparte, the emperor's brother, during his brief sojourn as king in Amsterdam (1806–10). Today, Queen Beatrix uses the palace only a few times a year, to welcome visiting dignitaries and for state receptions, preferring to live in the Huis ten Bosch on the outskirts of The Hague. The Dam Palace fronts straight onto the bustling square—no laid-out gardens or vistas were possible in this crowded, space-means-money business centre. Above the

On Queen's Day, fun-seeking Amsterdammers throng Dam Square before Royal Palace and New Church. Summing up mood, clowns frolic.

wide gable of the tympanum stands a Virgin of Peace statue and, behind her, the domed carillon bell tower (still playing tunes to the crowds below), installed by the world-famous campanologist brothers François and Pierre Hemony. The palace's interior is well worth a visit (see p. 57).

Just across the narrow Mozes en Aäronstraat stands the **Nieuwe Kerk** (New Church). This simple, late-Gothic basilica, whose origins

date back to the 15th century, was built without a tower (the willowy, miniature, neo-Gothic steeple was added in the mid-19th century). The church's glory is its baroque wood-carving and 16th- and 17th-century organs. An extensive restoration programme was carried out in the 1970s and all these attractions are open to the general public.

Statesmen and heroes from every walk of life (for example, Admiral de Ruyter and the

poet Joost van den Vondel) are buried in the Nieuwe Kerk, and Holland's monarchs are sworn in here.

The white, stone column on the other side of the square is the National Monument, erected by subscription in 1956 to commemorate the Dutch role in World War II. In a small curved wall at the back of the monument there are 12 urns—11 filled with soil from each Dutch province, and the twelfth with soil from Indonesia.

A few hundred yards behind the palace is the **Westerkerk** (West Church). Begun in 1619 by Hendrick de Keyser and finished in neo-classical style after his death by Jacob van Campen, it's distinguished not only by its tower—Amsterdam's tallest at 273 feet—but also by the shining, multicoloured crown with an orb on top, a replica of the crown presented to the city by Holy Roman Emperor Maximilian I in 1489.

The interior is spacious, but Calvinistically spartan in atmosphere. The church's organ was added in the 1680s, its panels painted by de Lairesse, a Rembrandt pupil. A plaque on the north wall records the fact that Rembrandt was buried in the church, but ex-

actly where he lies is not known.

The energetic visitor may like to climb the tower for an incomparable **view** of the city. Aloft, the carillon of 47 bells, some cast by François Hemony, strikes out merry tunes each half-hour of the day *and* night. If you're staying in a hotel nearby, you'll remember the tunes for years.

The **Anne Frankhuis** (Anne Frank House) is just around the corner at Prinsengracht 263. Here, for the two years from 1942 to 1944, this young Jewish girl hid from the Nazis, writing her now-famous diary. At the top of the steep stairway you can still see the bookcase wall which apparently closes off a corridor, but which in fact swings out and gives access to the secret *achterhuis,* or concealed part of the house behind, where Anne, her family and four friends eked out an existence until they were betrayed just nine months before war's end (see also MUSEUMS, pp. 53–60).

The **Jordaan** area, across the canal, lies between the west

Tower of West Church offers one of city's finest panoramic views.

the round Lutheran Church, opposite, into an annexe now used as a grand banqueting hall and reception/conference area.

Organ concerts are held under the 62-foot-diameter dome, and Sunday concerts at 11 a.m., ranging from jazz to police bands, operatic recitals to chamber music, have become a popular part of Amsterdam's weekend life.

For a change of perspective, head north, now, along the

Below: the round Sonesta Koepel.

Singel Canal and under the railway lines to the Havengebouw (harbour building) just west of the railway station. From the top of the building there is a superb **panoramic view** over Amsterdam. And if you feel in need of refreshment after sightseeing, there's a rooftop restaurant on the spot.

Central Section:

between Damrak and Oude Schans

Railway stations are rarely tourist sights, but Amsterdam's **central station,** dominating the Damrak boulevard vista, merits a moment of admiration as both a considerable engineering feat and a fine 19th-century neo-Gothic monument. It was built by Petrus Cuypers, architect also of the Rijksmuseum, on three artificial islands and 8,687 wooden piles.

At the waterfront opposite the station is the NZH (Noord-Zuid Hollands) Koffiehuis, a protected monument restored in 1981, housing the VVV tourist office and a restaurant.

Diagonally opposite the station over to your left is the St.-Nicolaaskerk (St. Nicholas' Church), where the Dutch counterpart to Santa Claus debarks in a mid-November ceremony to make his entry into the city (see p. 90).

Just a few yards down Damrak from the station, the former stock exchange building (the **Beurs van Berlage**), designed by Hendrik Petrus Berlage, has always excited controversy. It was one of Berlage's ultra-modern masterpieces when first unveiled to the world in 1903. Now it serves as a concert hall, home of the Dutch Philharmonic Orchestra. Exhibits on architecture are on show here as well.

The **Oude Kerk** (Old Church) is located just behind Beursplein and across Warmoesstraat.

This, the city's biggest and oldest church, was consecrated around 1300. It is the burial place of Rembrandt's wife Saskia. Though a wealth of decoration and statuary was disposed of by 17th-century Calvinists as "Catholic pomp", there remains a lot of Gothic stone carving to be admired both inside and outside, as well as some fine stained-glass including a window commemorating the Peace of Westphalia which, with the Peace of The Hague, brought an end to the 80-year Spanish War in 1648.

Squeezed bizarrely between student hostels and a couple of sex shops, the Old Church is in the middle of the red-light district. The centre of this area, popularly known in Dutch as the *walletjes* or "little walls", is in the parallel Oudezijds Voorburgwal, Oudezijds Achterburgwal and the Zeedijk, where sex shops, live sex shows and sex museums have blossomed in recent years. It's perfectly safe to stroll around—except perhaps in the early hours—and is, in fact, a prime tourist attraction; the ladies will ignore you if you ignore them.

Museum Amstelkring, otherwise known as Ons' Lieve Heer Op Solder (Our Lord in the Attic Church), at Oudezijds Voorburgwal 40, is the only one of Amsterdam's 60 once-clandestine Catholic churches of the Calvinist era left in the original condition. Tucked away up a series of steep stairs and winding corridors, it contains numerous relics of interest from the 18th century (see also Museums, pp. 53–60).

The 1482 **Schreierstoren** is across the small Chinese quarter of the lower Zeedijk. There is dispute over whether the tower's name derives from an old word meaning "to cry out", or from another word

meaning "astride". Certainly, the tower was built as a fortification point astride the Geldersekade canal on the old city harbour wall, but it was also the point of departure for sailors, and the legend of the Weeping Tower, or Tower of Tears, has more romantic appeal. Henry Hudson left from here to discover Manhattan in 1609, and a plaque commemorating the event is one of many on the tower.

Within sight of Schreierstoren lies the **Nederlands Scheepvaartmuseum** (Netherlands' Maritime Museum), appropriately blessed with a panoramic view of the harbour, and housed in vast old Admiralty supply buildings called 's Lands Zeemagazijn. It's full of model ships, charts, instruments and all the fascinating paraphernalia of sailing. For more details, see Museums, pp. 53–60.

The old **Montelbaanstoren** (Montelbaan Tower) on the Oude Schans canal, is said to be the city's best-proportioned tower. It was built as part of the 15th-century defences and bristled with cannon on its then flat roof. In 1606, the ar-

There's no escaping the city's sleazy, seedy, sexy side.

chitect Hendrick de Keyser added the present 143-foot spire, with clock and bells, in the same neo-classical style of his other towers.

The **Waag** (Weigh House) stands like a medieval, seven-turreted castle on Nieuwmarkt square. It was built in 1488 as a city gate, but as such was little used. It has had a varied career as weigh house, fire station, guildhouse, museum and, currently, multicultural information centre.

Guilds meeting there have included the stone-masons', which has left some intricate samples of its skill on both the outside and the inside of the building. Amsterdam's surgeons' guild held weekly anatomy lessons there in the 17th century and invited Rembrandt along to record the scene. The results were his two now world-famous paintings, both entitled *The Anatomy Lesson* (one *of Dr. Tulp,* the other *of Dr. Deijman*). All guilds

using the Weigh House had their own doorways, and these remain dotted around the building in an apparent confusion of entrances.

The nearby **Zuiderkerk** (South Church) was constructed between 1603 and 1611 by city architect Hendrick de Keyser, and its tower, added in 1614, has been its glory ever since. Because Christopher Wren admired it so much, it's said to have been the prototype for his many famous London steeples. Another noted figure was inspired to sketch and paint it —Rembrandt van Rijn, who lived opposite. There's a superb view of the tower from the small white drawbridge on the nearby Groenburgwal.

The brick-and-glass **Muziektheater** (Music Theatre) facing the River Amstel opened in 1986. The 1,600-seat theatre is home to the Netherlands Opera and the National Ballet. Because the building complex also includes the city's town hall *(stadhuis),* Amsterdammers have created the nickname "Stopera" *(stadhuis + opera).*

Waag (left) and Montelbaan Tower, once defensive positions in city walls, are now beloved landmarks.

The **Rembrandthuis** (Rembrandt's House) at Jodenbreestraat 4–6, red-shuttered and three storeys high, is a 1606 brick building with a typical Amsterdam step gable. It was the home of Holland's greatest painter from 1639 to his bankruptcy 20 years later. Here he lived, initially, in grand style, aided by his wife Saskia's 40,000-guilder dowry but also painting prolifically in an attempt to pay his way. Dating from this period are the *Anatomy Lesson of Dr. Deijman, Night Watch* and other works.

Jodenbreestraat, in which Rembrandt's house is located, means Jewish Broad Street, and you're now all set to take a closer look at the old Jewish quarter of town.

South-East Section:
between Waterlooplein and Rembrandtsplein

The **Portugees-Israëlitische Synagoge** (Portuguese synagogue) was built in 1675 by the city's large community of Sephardic Jews, descendants of refugees from Spain and Portugal in the late 16th century. It's said to have been patterned on the plan of King Solomon's temple. (The synagogue, on Jonas Daniël Meijer Square, is open irregularly.)

Adjoining the synagogue, the Ets Haim "Tree of Life" library dating from 1616 contains 20,000 books, prints and rare manuscripts highlighting Judaic history. The **Jewish Historical Museum** (see p. 60) also fronts on the square. Here, too, you'll see the **Dockworker Statue** by Mari Andriessen. Revered by Amsterdam Jew and Gentile alike, this rough figure of a man in working clothes commemorates the events of February 1941, when Amsterdam's dockworkers staged a 24-hour strike in protest against the deportation of Jews.

The cheery, impudent stallholders of Amsterdam's **fleamarket** on Waterlooplein will happily sell you anything from a fur coat to a twisted piece of lead piping, a fine old wind-up gramophone, cheap modern lock, solid oak table, century-old doll or—if you need one—a new shirt.

It's all bustle and bonhomie, with hardly any prices marked. In no matter what language the price question is asked, however, the stallholder's answer will be anything up to twice what he is eventually willing to take. It's the only

Blooming clogs wherever you
80 . . .

place in Amsterdam where you can really haggle. If the two of you finally can't agree, however, don't expect him to call you back. Your good-natured stallholder will by this time be a stubborn Dutchman who would rather lose cash than face.

Overlooking Waterlooplein is the **Mozes en Aäronkerk** (Moses and Aaron Church), an 1840 Catholic church with a name that again reflects the Jewish character of the area. It

has an imposing classical façade with a pillared entrance surmounted by a statue of Christ, and twin towers at each end of the balustraded roof. Two gablestones of "Moyses" and "Aaron" from an earlier church on this site are set into the wall.

Its festive, baroque-like interior looks down these days on scenes never envisaged by the church's founders. A meeting place for travelling youth, where they can buy soft drinks and snacks or stage art and craft exhibitions, it has also become a centre for foreign workers, who go there with their problems and attend

Sunday services specially designed for them.

The River Amstel, from which Amsterdam takes its name, is only a minute's walk away. For the best river view in town, cross the **Blaubrug** (Blue Bridge). Built in the 1880s and named after a former blue-painted wooden drawbridge on the site, it is a copy of the Pont Alexandre in Paris, richly ornamented with golden crowns and ships' prows.

Some consider it the city's most beautiful bridge, but look down-river to see its immediate rival, the white wooden drawbridge with nine graceful arches, the **Magere Brug,** or "Skinny Bridge", as it can be colloquially translated. This is unique and totally Amsterdam—a bottleneck for the single-file traffic but a delight for every photographer, especially in summer at dusk when, outlined with electric lights, it throws a perfect mirror-image onto the still water. By day at all times of the year the Skinny Bridge is a fascinating sight as it is regularly raised and lowered to allow passage to the busy barge traffic.

The name Magere is doubly significant: the bridge is indeed narrow, and magere in Dutch means thin or meagre, but the previous 17th-century bridge on this site was also paid for by two sisters coincidentally called Magere, who lived nearby.

Just beyond the Magere Brug, on the riverside, is the Carré Theatre, an attractive white stone building from 1887. Generally, it features Dutch-language shows, but sometimes visiting theatre and dance groups from abroad and pop shows perform.

The Willet Holthuysen Museum gardens will be on your left as you walk down narrow Amstelstraat. Like the museum itself (entrance on parallel Herengracht—see p. 60), they are in authentic 17th- and 18th-century style.

Rembrandtsplein (Rembrandt Square) and the adjoining Thorbeckeplein are Amsterdam's scaled-down version of Times Square, New York, or Leicester Square, London. Covered with advertising, cinema, restaurant, bar and night-club signs, they form a brash fun area offering everything from strip-shows and English-language films to

City flag flies on boat on River Amstel near Magere Brug, one of Amsterdam's 1,000 bridges. South Church tower rises in background.

a cup of coffee at one of the many outdoor cafés. The grassy centre of the square, with its benches, is a pleasant relief from the frenzy all around, particularly when the banks of rhododendron are in flower.

Utrechtsestraat, leading south out of the square, is fast developing into a major restaurant street.

A view of 14 bridges makes a tranquil finale to this active, four-section tour of town.

From the far end of Thorbeckeplein, look down Reguliersgracht to see six of them in a row. To the left down Herengracht are six more, and to the right another two. It's a particularly memorable view in summer after dark, when all the bridges are lit.

The best way to go is by bike, and there's always a handy bollard to solve parking problems.

Museums

Amsterdam's museums are generally open from 10 or 11 a.m. to 5 p.m. on weekdays (some close on Mondays) and from 1 to 5 p.m. on Sundays and public holidays. Prices of admission range from low to moderate. A special one-year ticket for all state museums in Holland as well as the municipal museums in Amsterdam is available at VVV tourist information offices on presentation of your passport.

Rijksmuseum

Luckily for the bewildered visitor to this vast (250 rooms) palace of a museum, an easy-to-follow ground plan, with an index of exhibits, is available at the information desk on the first floor* for a nominal sum.

If your main interest is European art, and Dutch painting in particular, head for the first floor, rooms 201–236.

Here, in room 224, Rembrandt's monumental *Night Watch* (properly entitled *The Company of Captain Frans*

_____
* The Netherlands follows general European usage in designating what an American calls the first floor the *ground* floor, his second floor the *first* floor, and so on upwards.

Banning Cocq and Lieutenant Willem van Ruytenburch) holds pride of place. Painted in 1642, when the artist was 37, it remains epic, slightly awe-inspiring and yet so warm in human terms.

The interplay of light and shadow is an important element in Rembrandt's work. Indeed, the members of Amsterdam's Civic Guard who had commissioned the *Night Watch,* and whom it portrays, criticized the painting for being too dashing, for playing about with light and for partially obscuring some of the subjects by its unconventional composition, and tucked it away on one of the least favourable walls of their new meeting hall.

Other highlights of Rembrandt's work on display in rooms 229 and 230 include the lustrous and tender *Loving Couple* (also called *The Jewish Bride*), the slightly comic *Self-Portrait as the Apostle Paul,* for which he donned a turban, and the *Staalmeesters,* one of his later works and one which confirms him again as one of the greatest group portrait painters of all time.

The effect and distribution of light also play an important part in the works of another great painter of the Netherlands' Golden Age, Jan Vermeer (1632–75). Nowhere is this better seen than in his *Young Woman Reading a Letter,* one of four of his works hanging in room 222, adjoining the *Night Watch* room.

Frans Hals (1580–1666) has two rooms to himself (209 and 210), and his superb portrait *The Merry Drinker* can be seen in room 214A.

Jacob van Ruisdael (c. 1628 –82), often considered the greatest landscape painter of his century, is represented, in room 214, by his *Mill near Wijk bij Duurstede* and *View of Haarlem,* among others.

Then, in rooms 216 and 218, there are several Jan Steens (1626–79), with their witty observations of family feastings; in room 216, idealized landscapes of Albert Cuyp (1620–

Rembrandt's Staalmeesters *in the Rijksmuseum; one of de Kooning's abstract works (right) in the Stedelijk.*

91); and, in various rooms, later Dutch work by Cornelius Troost, Jacob de Wit and many more.

Next to the *Night Watch* room is a large sectioned gallery given over to non-Dutch artists, grouped according to nationality. Here you'll find Rubens and the Brueghels, Botticelli, Fra Angelico and Tintoretto, Goya, El Greco and Velázquez.

To give more than a very general idea of the other, varied treasures that the Rijksmuseum contains is impossible here. Suffice it to say that whether your interests extend to porcelain, Asiatic or Muslim art, Dutch history, 18th-century glassware or 17th-century dolls' houses, to name but a few of the remaining exhibits, the Rijksmuseum has something for you.

Location: Stadhouderskade (backing onto Museumplein).

Stedelijk Museum

The Stedelijk's collection of famous names is as impressive, in its own field, as the Rijksmuseum's. Picasso is represented by *Still Life with Guitar, Glass with Straws* and *Sitting Woman with Fish Hat;* Monet, Degas and Cézanne are there, Matisse, Mondrian and de Kooning. But look

especially for Chagall. His *Man with Violin* is unforgettably serio-comic and colourful.

Special exhibitions are constantly being mounted, and the Stedelijk's catholic taste embraces most things from trams to Andy Warhol.

Location: Paulus Potterstraat 13 (on Museumplein).

Vincent van Gogh Museum

This modern, 1973 building houses in its airy light over 200 paintings and 400 drawings by **55** van Gogh (1853–90), plus a room of such contemporaries as Toulouse-Lautrec and Vincent's sometime friend, Gauguin.

There are a few sketches from his London days when as a young man he fell in love, and despaired when he was jilted. Still-lifes and peasant scenes, including his first masterpiece, *The Potato Eaters,* represent his early Dutch period. Through Antwerp and Paris (no fewer than 11 self-portraits, when he was too

Van Gogh's dazzling paintings attract millions to his museum.

poor to pay models), and then to Arles, where he painted in a compulsive frenzy. From those 15 months of joy and madness came a priceless genius now comprehensively on view here: his series of blossom paintings, wheatfields, orchards and sunflowers. Moving on to a mental

clinic in Saint-Rémy, he remembered his bedroom at Arles, and this, too, is one of the famed paintings displayed.

Apart from his canvases and a gallery of his painted Japanese woodcuts, which he much admired, the museum also houses hundreds of letters from Vincent, his family and friends.

Location: Paulus Potterstraat 7 (on Museumplein).

Rembrandthuis (Rembrandt's House). The painter's home from riches to rags, fame to bankruptcy, was restored in his memory in 1906 and contains 350 of his etchings (including *The Jewish Bride*) as well as his own etching press.

Location: Jodenbreestraat 4–6.

Koninklijk Paleis (Royal Palace). The huge, classic interior of this 17th-century town-hall-turned-royal-residence contains a mass of sculpted symbolism executed by Artus Quellinus the Elder and others and some of the finest Empire furniture in the world, left behind by Louis Bonaparte when he fled the city overnight in 1810 (see p. 19). In the massive 97-foot-high Civic Hall, Quellinus's work looks down on an inlaid mosaic floor of celestial and terrestrial globes fit, indeed, for a king to walk on. Paintings include contributions by Ferdinand Bol, one of Rembrandt's pupils, and specially commissioned works by the artist Govert Flinck.

Location: Dam Square.

Hours: (provided the palace is not in use) summer months: 12.30 p.m. to 4 p.m. daily. Winter months: guided tour Wednesday at 2 p.m.

Amsterdams Historisch Museum (Amsterdam Historical Museum): In the heart of the city, a comprehensive look, in beautiful 17th-century surroundings, at Amsterdam 1275–1945. More classic Dutch painting here, but mainly a rich and beautifully arranged collection of items pertaining to Amsterdam's history (see also p. 35).

Location: Kalverstraat 92.

Nederlands Scheepvaartmuseum (Dutch Maritime Museum). Several hundred detailed model ships head the list of exhibits in this museum to please all age groups. Paintings, prints, countless maps, globes and a library of 60,000 volumes—many from the 16th and 17th centuries—

arouse the imagination. Look carefully and you'll see the certificate of purchase that American Indians gave to Dutch merchant Peter Minuit for land around Albany, New York, in 1631, and the oldest known depiction of New York City, in 1656.

Location: Kattenburgerplein 1.

Tropenmuseum (Tropical Museum). Renovated and modernized, this exceptionally interesting museum provides a vivid insight into folk art, costumes, products and way of life, with an emphasis on South-East Asia. It also contains a wealth of material from Africa, India and South America. A special children's section is guaranteed to fascinate the youngsters.

Most Sunday afternoons, the museum sponsors performances of folk song, dance and drama from various parts of the tropical world—a pleasant (free) extra.

Location: Linnaeusstraat 2.

Anne Frankhuis (Anne Frank House). In this 1635 building, see the rooms where Anne and her family hid for two years from the occupying Nazi troops, between 1942 and 1944. The stove they used is still there, as well as poignant magazine cuttings of her favourite stars, stuck on the bedroom wall by this 15-year-old who did not survive—but left an incomparable diary for the world. Since it first appeared in 1947, more than 4 million copies in 33 languages have been printed (see also p. 38).

Folk dance sometimes enlivens the scene at the Amsterdam Historical Museum.

Location: Prinsengracht 263.
Hours: Monday to Saturday, 9 a.m. to 5 p.m.; Sunday, 10 a.m. to 5 p.m.

Bijbels Museum (Biblical Museum and Workshop). In addition to a unique Judaeo-Christian exhibition aiming to show what it was like to live in Palestine around the time of Christ, children are encouraged to paint and draw here, to make models, play musical instruments—even

to act out plays on biblical themes.

Location: Herengracht 368.

Museum Amstelkring (also known as Ons' Lieve Heer Op Solder, meaning "Our Lord in the Attic"). This clandestine Catholic church from the Calvinist era is at the top of three 1661–63 homes in one of the most colourful parts of the city. Its 17th- and 18th-century exhibits include a 1794 organ which is still used at weddings and a hinged pulpit which can be tucked away out of sight to save space.

Location: Oudezijds Voorburgwal 40.

Museum Willet Holthuysen. Built in 1689 as a private residence for an eminent *burgher,* this house still has a family atmosphere and great authenticity. It is, in many respects, a perfect example of a patrician Amsterdam house. There's also a fine family art collection.

Location: Herengracht 605.

Madame Tussaud's. A branch of the renowned London waxworks, with international figures looking chillingly lifelike and some Dutch personalities for local colour—soccer stars, comedians, singers and, naturally, Rembrandt in his studio.

Location: Kalverstraat 156.

Aviodome. Here's the story of flight from the 18th-century Montgolfier brothers of France, who invented the hot-air balloon, to the Viking mission to Mars, including a Sputnik given by the Soviet Union, and a Link trainer which simulates flying, and on which visitors can take a ten-minute test.

Location: Schiphol airport.

Zeiss Planetarium Amsterdam. Settle down comfortably and watch the stars appear and disappear in the artificial "sky" overhead. All in the space of a few minutes, you see day passing into night and night into day, the different phases of the moon and the motion of the planets throughout the year.

Location: Zoo Artis.

Joods Historisch Museum (Jewish Historical Museum). An impressive collection of holy Jewish objects, as well as a record of the World War II occupation.

Location: Jonas Daniël Meijerplein.

Dutch Masters, Old and New

Holland's glorious 17th century produced an amazing array of brilliant painters. Among the most outstanding were:

FRANS HALS (c. 1580–1666) is often considered the founder of the Dutch School. He's particularly noted for portraits and groups. *The Laughing Cavalier* demonstrates his gift for giving his subjects a lively, even sprightly, air.

REMBRANDT HARMENSZ VAN RIJN (1606–69) is the undisputed giant of Dutch painting and ranks among the greatest of all time. Born in Leiden, he acquired fame and fortune (and later fell into ignominy and bankruptcy) in Amsterdam. His revolutionary use of light and shade, and genius in group portraits, is best seen in his *Night Watch*.

JACOB VAN RUISDAEL (c. 1628–82) is the great master of the landscape. He's known for the vivid scenes he painted of his native Haarlem, as true to life as a photograph, and for moody interpretations of the Dutch countryside.

JAN STEEN (1626–79) specialized in domestic interiors and lively tavern scenes. He's associated with several towns—The Hague, Delft, Haarlem and Leyden, where he kept a tavern.

JAN VERMEER (1632–75) was born and died in Delft and as far as anyone knows, never left the town. His delicate interiors glow in subtle hues of gold.

After a decline in the 18th and early 19th centuries, Dutch painting saw a new upsurge in the late 1800s.

VINCENT VAN GOGH (1853–90) moved from provincial Holland to London, Antwerp and Paris before spending most of his last two years in Arles, in the south of France. His art is inseparable from his tormented inner life.

PIET MONDRIAAN, or Mondrian (1872–1944), born in Amersfoort, near Amsterdam, spent many years in Paris before moving to London, Arizona and New York, where he died. His abstract paintings, consisting often of stark rectangles in primary colours, represent the reduction of an object to its most basic, underlying essence.

WILLEM DE KOONING was born in Rotterdam in 1904. He settled in the United States in 1926, where he developed his own brand of abstract expressionism, notably in the lurid *Woman* series.

Excursions

Amsterdam is the capital of a small country, and it's possible to leave the city behind in ten minutes. Your first windmill might soon appear and, as soon as you get onto a secondary road, your first farmer cycling along in yellow wooden shoes.

Within an hour you can get to many other major Dutch cities (for example: The Hague is 57 kilometres away, Haarlem 19, Delft 61 and Rotterdam 73).

Several bus companies run a series of extremely well-organized daily excursions. If your hotel doesn't have their brochures, you'll find them at the tourist office opposite the main railway station. Or, if you're motorized and prefer to go it alone, you may

Weekend sailors set forth in boat patterned on traditional model.

like to choose from the excursions in the following pages which describe some of the different faces of Holland.

Yet how many other eminently interesting towns are there within easy reach of the capital! Among them, but outside the scope of this book, is Rotterdam, this phoenix of a city risen from the ashes of World War II destruction. From its generously laid-out traffic-free shopping precincts to the dizzying heights of the 185-metre-high Euromast with its view of the city's huge, bustling port, Rotterdam symbolizes the Dutch will, not only to survive adversity but also to thrive—hallmarks of Dutch resoluteness seen everywhere in this remarkable land wrested from the sea.

By the Side of the Zuyder Zee*

Leave Amsterdam by the IJ-tunnel, and within ten minutes you'll be in the utter calm of **Broek in Waterland.** With its narrow streets and wooden houses, as distinct from the red-brick homes usually found in Holland, its tiny lake and profusion of waterfowl, this claims to be the prettiest Dutch village of them all.

Marken, shortly to the east, is a former island now linked to the mainland by a causeway. A Calvinist village with a closed community that strictly keeps the Sabbath, its very distinctive local costume is still widely worn. The village has a colourful and genuine old harbour and lots of photogenic houses painted green and white or pitch black. In spite of its popularity with tourists, Marken has preserved much of its authenticity and charm.

Back on the mainland, you will soon reach MONNICKENDAM, a former Zuyder Zee harbour with a colourful modern port, an impressive late-Gothic church with stained-glass windows, a slender 16th-century tower with carillon and a variety of 17th-century gabled houses.

Next stop is **Volendam,** a Catholic counterpart to Marken, visible across the water. The harbour and main street on top of the dike are crowded with visitors looking for costumed locals to be photographed alongside them. You can even hire a costume for your snapshot!

---

* The old Zuyder Zee was renamed the IJsselmeer after completion of the barrier dam which cut it off from the North Sea.

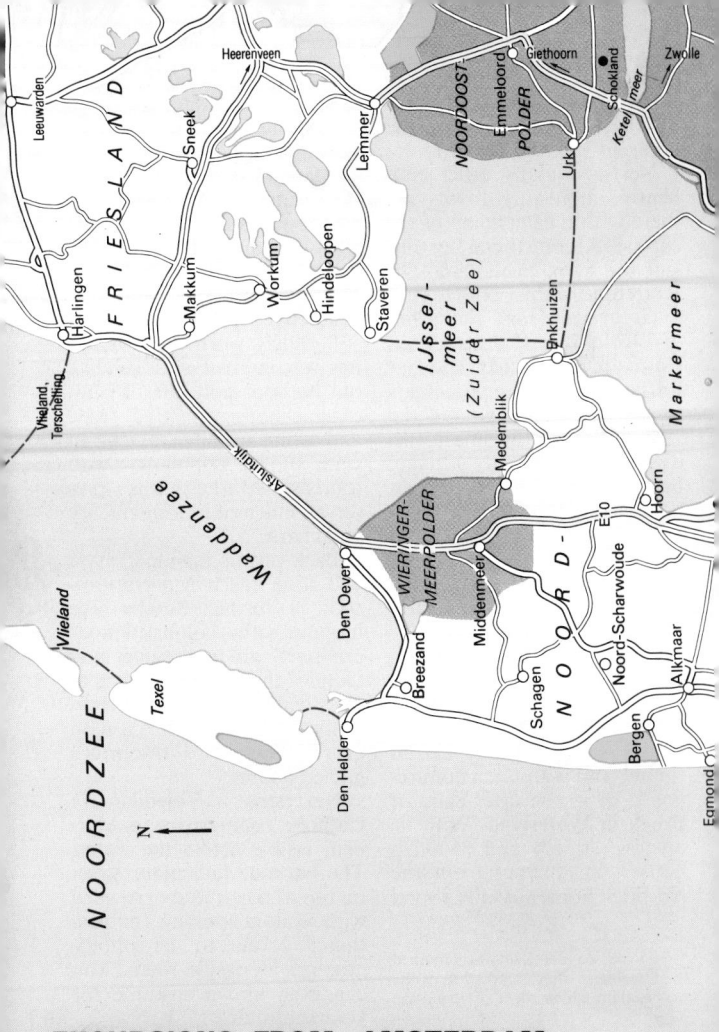

EXCURSIONS FROM AMSTERDAM

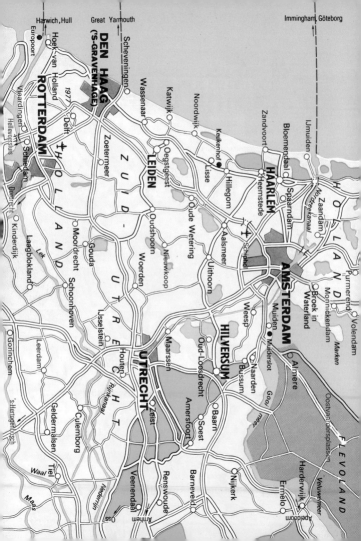

The town of **Edam** is miraculously unspoilt despite its well-known name. Its famous cheese is still made at farms in the vicinity. A unique 17th-century town centre is dominated by the Damsluis, a vaulted and paved-over lock, and the town hall, in Louis XIV-style. Overlooking the

Traditional costumes are worn in waterside village of Marken, among the region's most scenic.

bridge is the Kapiteinshuis (Captain's House), dating from 1540, now an interesting museum with a "floating cellar".

Also in Edam is a cheese weigh house *(Kaaswaag),* again from the 17th century, displaying old cheese-making equipment and selling cheese.

From Edam it's 20 kilometres to **Hoorn,** once one of the home ports of the Dutch East Indies Company; many of its rich merchants' houses

and public buildings from the Golden Age have been preserved. It was from here that several early Dutch explorers set sail, among them Willem Schouten, who, in 1616, first rounded Cape Horn (he named it Kaap Hoorn).

The road leads on to another jewel—**Enkhuizen.** In the old days, great, three-masted East-Indiamen would be lying offshore, having rounded the tip of Den Helder for the comparative calm of the Zuyder Zee. Today, it's a boat and fishing harbour, still quaintly controlled by the 16th-century Drommedaris, a fortified tower, now a town cultural centre. You can climb to the top of the tower for a wonderful wiew of the IJsselmeer. The indoor section of the fascinating **Zuyder Zee Museum** is located in a 1625 warehouse. Next to it, but only attainable by boat, is the open-air section, a magnificent collection of typical Zuyder Zee houses, farms and workshops, illustrating life as it was between 1880 and 1932. One ticket covers entry to both sections as well as the boat fare. The boat departs every 15 minutes from the railway station and from the car park.

Heading back, now, towards Amsterdam, there's an inter-

esting side-trip to be made to the pretty town of ALKMAAR. Indeed, if you're making this trip on a Friday between mid-April and mid-September, you may well be tempted to reverse the whole order of the excursion and make Alkmaar your first visit. The reason is Alkmaar's weekly cheese market, held at this time of year in the market-place between 10 a.m. and noon.

These Friday mornings, wholesalers converge to test

the cheese and then to bid at the auction. Afterwards, the Cheese Porters, two by two, carry as many as 80 cannon-ball-shaped Edam cheeses or 12 disc-shaped Gouda cheeses on special barrows to the weigh house.

There are four companies of cheese porters, all dressed in spotless white. Their straw hats are lacquered green, blue, red or yellow, to denote which company they belong to.

South of Alkmaar, on the river Zaan, try to stop at another delightful open-air museum, **Zaanse Schans,** with wooden houses that are inhabited, a grocery that sells traditional sweets and a variety of windmills that are still operational. In addition, there is a clock museum, an old-time bakery and a wooden shoe workshop.

Round the IJsselmeer

This trip will give you a first-hand insight into the impressive achievements of Dutch land reclamation represented by the 30-kilometre barrier dam *(Afsluitdijk)* which, in 1932, transformed the huge tidal gulf of the Zuyder Zee into the freshwater lake now named the IJsselmeer, with its spacious polders (stretches of reclaimed sea-bed).

After the IJtunnel leading out of Amsterdam, follow the E10 highway and the signs for Leeuwarden.

You'll reach MIDDENMEER on your way north without even suspecting that you've already penetrated deep into the oldest of the reclaimed Zuyder Zee polders, the Wieringermeer, completed in 1930 and put to agricultural use in 1935.

At the eastern tip of the former island of Wieringen lies the little port of DEN OEVER, its locks and sluices linking the IJsselmeer with the North Sea. Here begins the **Afsluitdijk,** a truly amazing feat of hydraulic engineering.

In front of you, stretching as far as the eye can see, is a four-lane highway built defiantly on huge blocks of stone against the wrath of the North Sea to your left. Seven kilometres along is a café and lookout tower where the last section of the dike was put into place against tremendous water pressure that almost washed it away again. Explanatory plaques describe the composition and building schedule of the barrage.

Leaving the dike, you're in the province of Friesland, an area with its own customs and culture and even its own language, Frisian.

Alkmaar's colourful guild helps put Dutch cheese on the market.

Just a few miles south of the dike is **Makkum,** home of one of Holland's most famous potteries for more than 300 years (see pp. 85–86).

Fifteen kilometres down the coast is another village for the arts and crafts enthusiast— **Hindeloopen.** Here the speciality since the 16th century has been brightly coloured, hand-painted rustic furniture decorated with intricate designs of flowers and intertwining leaves.

South now to EMMELOORD and a fascinating little side-trip (30 kilometres each way) east to GIETHOORN, a village with no streets—only canals —where even the milkman goes by punt.

From Emmeloord, the main road south-west is signposted to Lelystad and Amsterdam. Already you're on land reclaimed after the Afsluitdijk **69**

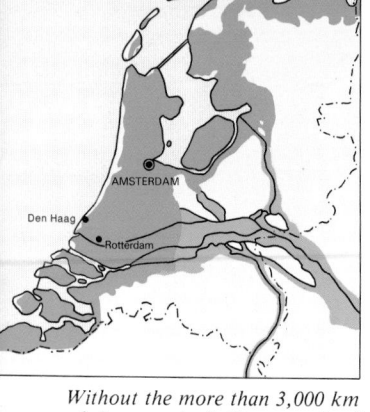

Without the more than 3,000 km of dunes and of dikes, much of the country would be flooded, as shown above, by the sea (dark green) or rivers (light green).

Land Below the Sea

As early as the 12th century, Dutch monasteries began reclaiming land from the sea. The technique is basically simple: lakes and estuaries are ringed with dikes, and the water is then pumped out into canals, from which it flows into rivers and out to sea. Each unit of newly reclaimed land is called a polder.

The job of keeping the country's feet dry is never-ending. Rising groundwater within the polder must be continuously controlled by pumping stations.

Today, 60 per cent of Holland's 15 million inhabitants live on land wrested from the sea and protected by more than 3,000 kilometres of dunes and dikes. Where jumbo jets now taxi at Schiphol Airport, a sea battle was once fought against the Spanish on the 18,000-hectare lake which then covered the area. The completed IJsselmeer polders have added nearly 5 per cent to the nation's land area.

In February 1953, an unusually violent gale combined with an exceptional spring tide to breach the dikes in a score of places. Widespread loss of life, devastation of property and

was finally closed. This is the 120,000-acre Noordoost (North-East) polder, completed in 1942 and the oldest of the three you will now drive across. Everything looks so developed here, yet only 40 years ago this land was the bottom of the sea.

Down the road from Emmeloord are signposts pointing right to Urk, left to Schokland. Before reclamation, both were islands jutting a few feet above the Zuyder Zee.

The former island of URK is now a fishing village on the edge of the mainland. The

flooding of agricultural land were the tragic consequences. To prevent any recurrence of this kind of disaster, the Dutch have now closed off the major sea arms of the Waal (Rhine) delta. The Delta Plan is another major feat of Dutch hydraulic engineering.

Starkly geometric layout of fields betrays their origin as reclaimed polder land (here East Flevoland).

busy fleet now gets out into the North Sea via the sluice gates at Den Oever.

As you drive down towards Amsterdam, you'll notice the different stages of development of the two Flevoland polders, the Oostelijk (East) Flevoland, which was completed in 1957—already widely cultivated—and the contiguous Zuidelijk (South) Flevoland, drained in 1968, looking "emptier" and "newer" with its Lego-like farms. Between

Lelystad and Almere lies an uncultivated area, the Oostvaardersplassen. Wild and marshy, it is a paradise for birds.

On your right, you'll see a 30-kilometre-long dike, stretching across the IJsselmeer to Enkhuizen and intended to close off another polder under study. It provides a fast road connection between Flevoland and North Holland.

Shortly after Almere, a bridge connects Flevoland to the mainland. Beyond, in the direction of Amsterdam, stands the forbidding **Castle of Muiden** *(Muiderslot),* first built in the 13th century. Count Floris V was murdered there in 1296. One of only two unaltered medieval castles in Holland, it now houses a historical museum.

Wayside poppets sell tulips. New sculpture (opposite) contrasts with Renaissance Vleeshal in Haarlem.

Haarlem and the Tulip Trail
Pop. 150,000
(Amsterdam, 19 km.)

A treasure-house of historical buildings, Haarlem's centre is dominated, even overawed, by the massive **St.-Bavokerk.** Inside this 15th-century monument is one of the finest church organs in Europe, a three-manual instrument with 5,000 pipes, installed in 1738. Both Mozart and Handel played on it, and you can hear the quality for yourself during resitals held on Thursdays at 3 p.m. from mid-May to August.

The **Vleeshal** (meat market) opposite the church is one of Holland's finest Renaissance buildings. And then there's the **Frans Hals Museum** devoted to the town's most famous son (1580–1666). Eleven of his paintings are assembled there, and the house itself is a gem, dating from 1608 and with a beautifully preserved 17th-century garden.

At the height of summer you might like to continue on to ZANDVOORT for a dip in the bracing North Sea. In August, banners herald the *grand prix* car race, while at any time of the year you can try your luck in the town's casino. From mid-April to the end of May

the floral route to the south of Haarlem beckons.

Never in your life will you have seen as many tulips and other cultivated flowers as the thousands of hectares down through HEEMSTEDE and HIL-LEGOM to LISSE, all planted in flawless rectangles according to colour. Just before Lisse is the 28-hectare **Keukenhof**, a showpiece flower garden which, for two months from the end of March, successively focuses on crocus, hyacinth

73

and narcissus displays, then on early- and late-blooming tulips.

From Lisse it's only a short drive to the huge **cut-flower auction hall** *(Bloemenveiling)* at Legmeerdijk, near AALS-MEER, where millions of roses, carnations, freesias, lilacs and other blooms are sold during the year. Visitors are admitted Monday to Friday from 7.30 to 11 a.m.

Leiden
Pop. 110,000
(Amsterdam, 40 km.)
This old university town, birthplace of Rembrandt and Jan Steen, can be conveniently visited as an extension to a trip to Haarlem and the bulb country or as a stop on the way to The Hague, Delft or Rotterdam.

The tourist information office at Stationsplein 210, opposite the railway station, is a good place to start from. You might first like to visit the tall windmill, **De Valk,** only a few hundred metres away. It dates from 1743 and contains a fine collection of miller's equipment. If the wind is suitable, the mill is put in operation. (Closed on Mondays.)

The **Lakenhal,** on Oude Singel, former guildhall of the town's clothmakers, was built in 1639. It now houses the city museum's historical and decorative-arts collection, as well as oils by the Renaissance painter Lucas van Leyden and others.

The nearby Rijksmuseum voor Volkenkunde (Ethnographic Museum) is rich in exhibits from outside Europe.

At the back of the museum's garden stands a 17th-century town gate, the Morspoort, and near it a rebuilt windmill.

Breestraat is the busy main street of the **old town.** Up here, on the left-hand side, is the splendid Renaissance façade of the Stadhuis (town hall), the only part of the original building to survive a disastrous fire in 1929. The first turning left after this will bring you to a **covered bridge,** built in 1642, which commands some delightful views.

Beyond the bridge lies the historical heart of the old town, the artificial fortified hillock called the **Burcht** that dates from the 12th century. Some of the town's oldest and finest almshouses, not to mention the 14th-century Hooglandse Kerk (St. Pancras' Church), grace this area.

The massive, Gothic **St.-Pieterskerk** stands out to the

west of Breestraat. It was consecrated in 1121, though not completed until the early 15th century. Here John Robinson, one of the spiritual leaders of the Pilgrim Fathers, lies buried. One of the outer walls bears a plaque in his memory.

In Kloksteeg, opposite this plaque, is the **Jan Pesijnhofje,** another of those attractive clusters of almshouses for which Leiden is famous. This one was founded in 1683 by an ancestor of President Franklin D. Roosevelt.

Kloksteeg leads down to the pretty **Rapenburg Canal,** across which lies the **Academie,** the main building of the university. Founded in 1575 by William the Silent as a reward for the town's valiant resistance to a protracted Spanish siege, the Academie still looks virtually the same as it did 400 years ago. The flourishing Botanical Garden behind it dates from the same period.

Turn right at the bottom of Kloksteeg and follow the Rapenburg Canal. At No. 28, the Rijksmuseum voor Oudheden (National Antiquities Museum) houses the country's finest collection of Egyptian mummies and hieroglyphic inscriptions.

The Hague
Pop. 444,000
(Amsterdam, 57 km.)
Den Haag, or The Hague, is Holland's diplomatic city and seat of government, as well as the home of the International Court of Justice. Though Amsterdam is the capital city, The Hague claims the glories of court and government.

Undoubtedly, the jewel of The Hague is the **Binnenhof,** now the seat of Parliament. Monumental gateways provide access to a rectangular courtyard lined with government buildings. The magnificent medieval **Ridderzaal,** or Knights' Hall, which dates back to the 13th century, stands at the heart of the Binnenhof. Supported by great beams and adorned by stained-glass windows, it emanates a sense of history. It's here that the Queen arrives each September in her golden coach to open Parliament. The Ridderzaal is considered one of the finest Gothic buildings in northern Europe. Guided tours are available year-round from Monday to Saturday from 10 a.m. to 3.55 p.m. and, in July and August, on Sundays from noon to 4 p.m. as well.

For a different perspective on the old days, visit the Gevangenpoort ("Prison Gate") museum at Buitenhof 33, with its rather gruesome exhibition of torture instruments. Guided tours Monday to Friday from 11 a.m. to 4 p.m. Saturdays, Sundays and public holidays from 1 p.m.

As you walk around the Hofvijver, the square pond next to the Binnenhof, you'll notice some very elegant 18th-century houses on Lange Vijverberg. At the far end of the pond, at Korte Vijverberg 7, is the Haags Historisch Museum, with an interesting collection on the history of the town.

Bordering on the pond is the **Mauritshuis,** a residence constructed by the Dutch ex-governor of northern Brazil from 1637 to 1644. Now, it houses one of the world's finest small art collections. Among its 400 or so paintings are several Rembrandts, Vermeer's *View of Delft* and a number of works by Jan Steen, Frans Hals and others. Open Tuesday to Saturday from 10 a.m. to 5 p.m., Sundays and public holidays from 11 a.m.

Across the Hofvijver lies the most distinguished quarter of The Hague: the rectangle formed by Kneuterdijk, Lange Vijverberg and Lange Voorhout. The **Lange Voorhout,** in particular—a broad avenue with three double rows of lime trees, lined with stately 17th- and 18th-century houses, some of which are now in use as embassies—has a specific stylish character of its own.

Don't miss **Panorama Mesdag,** at Zeestraat 65b, which gives a detailed picture of what The Hague's seaside neighbour, Scheveningen, looked like in 1881. The circular painting that lines the walls gives you the optical illusion of standing on top of a dune, enjoying a 360° view.

Close by, at Zeestraat 82, the Nederlands Postmuseum (Dutch Postal Museum) contains an interesting exhibition of the country's postal history and equipment.

From here it's only a short walk to the **Vredespaleis** (Peace Palace) at Carnegieplein. Financed by the Scottish-American steel tycoon Andrew Carnegie, this is the

---

76

THE HAGUE – CITY CENTRE

seat of the International Court of Justice and related bodies.

Guided tours are from Monday to Friday at 10 and 11 a.m. and 2 and 3 p.m. The palace may be closed when the court

Historic government buildings line the Hofvijver in The Hague. Right: Delft New Church, market-place.

Monet and van Gogh and sculptures by Henry Moore and Barbara Hepworth. Other exhibits include a vast collection of musical instruments, both European and oriental.

The adjacent Museon is a modern museum covering various facets of culture, science and technology.

is in session. It is best to call before going: 070-346 96 80.

The **Haagse Gemeentemuseum** (Municipal Museum) on Stadhouderslaan contains the world's largest collection of paintings by the Dutch neoplastic artist Piet Mondriaan (1872–1944, see p. 61), in addition to works by Picasso,

Children especially, but not exclusively, will love the miniature city of **Madurodam**. On its 16,000 square metres, some 150 of Holland's most famous buildings are reproduced at 1/25th actual size. Trains and planes are there, too. At dusk, 50,000 tiny lights twinkle in its streets. Madurodam even has a mayoress and a council consisting of 32 local school children, annually elected. It opens daily at 9 a.m. and closes at 11 p.m. (June–August), 9.30 p.m. (September), 6 p.m. (October–January 6) or 10.30 p.m. (March–May).

Interested in the trappings of royalty? The Queen lives in a delightful palace in the eastern outskirts of The Hague, Huis ten Bosch, surrounded by lovely woodlands.

Her office is in another palace, on Noordeinde, considered to be Holland's most elegant shopping street.

To round off your busy trip to The Hague, what better than a walk along the sands at the famous seaside resort of **Scheveningen,** with its impressive pier and the Kurhaus spa hotel with its casino, Europe's biggest.

WASSENAAR, just north of The Hague, is one of Holland's most prestigious residential areas. It boasts some beautifully laid-out gardens, although most are hidden among the trees.

Delft
Pop. 88,000
(Amsterdam, 61 km.)
About halfway between The Hague and Rotterdam, and

Holland's windmills once played a vital role in draining the land.

some 15 minutes' drive from either, lies Delft, one of Holland's most picturesque towns —home of the distinctive blue and white pottery that bears its name. But tradition and conservation haven't hampered Delft's development as an important industrial centre and home of a great technological university.

In summer, you can give your tired feet a rest by taking a tour by boat (leaving from Koornmarkt) on Delft's tree-lined canals spanned by graceful, high-vaulted bridges.

The canals are flanked by attractive 17th- and 18th-century houses, and the focal point of Delft is its spacious **marketplace,** one of the country's most charming.

At its western end stands the Renaissance **Raadhuis** (town hall), but the elongated square

Windmill Country

Holland's windmills, now a decorative feature of the landscape, were once essential to the country's survival. Without drainage mills, water could not have been cleared from below sea level throughout the whole of North Holland. The countryside would still be laced with lakes.

Most of the surviving 950 mills throughout the country are protected as monuments, and some 200 of them are still in use. Concentrations of them or unusual varieties can be seen:

At Arnhem's Open-air Museum (Openluchtmuseum), 96 km. south-east of Amsterdam, all major types of mills have been preserved.

At Zaanse Schans Open-air Museum near Zaandam, 16 km. north-west of Amsterdam, there are several different types, including a saw mill, a paint mill and an oil mill.

At Schiedam, just west of Rotterdam, there are still four out of the original 18 tall stone mills which formerly dotted its ramparts.

But the most impressive line-up of windmills is to be found at Kinderdijk, some 20 km. east of Rotterdam. Here, there are 19 mills, 17 of which turn their sails together on Saturday afternoons in July and August. At least one can be seen in operation every weekday from April to October.

Like every other Dutch town, Amsterdam bristled with windmills centuries ago. Today there are six left, one serving as a suburban restaurant, another on a grassy bank overlooking the river Amstel on the southern edge of town—an excellent location for holiday snapshots.

is dominated by the **Nieuwe Kerk** (New Church). Begun in 1384, it took more than 100 years to build. It is the final resting place of William the Silent, founder of the nation, and of many other members of the House of Orange.

Behind the town hall, the old Boterhuis (butter market) and Waag (weigh house) can still be seen. Leave the marketplace here, cross over Wijnhaven, walk along Boterbrug—street and bridge in one—and you'll come upon the Oude Delft Canal, almost 1,000 years old.

About 150 metres to the right are two more of the town's landmarks, the Oude Kerk and the Prinsenhof.

The **Oude Kerk** (Old Church) was begun in the first part of the 13th century, and has been renovated on several occasions since. Note its heavy leaning tower with straightened turrets.

The **Prinsenhof,** formerly a convent, became the residence of William the Silent in 1572. Twelve years later, he was murdered here by a hired assassin in the pay of the Spanish King Philip II. The bullet holes—greatly enlarged by the probing fingers of early visitors—can still be seen near the foot of a winding staircase.

Part of the Prinsenhof is now given over to a museum devoted to the Dutch War of Independence (1568–1648). It also includes a number of paintings, banners and other objects pertaining to various members of the House of Orange, as well as an interesting collection of silver. Every summer, an antique fair is held here. Since the date is movable, check with any Dutch tourist office if you're interested in attending.

Just beyond the Prinsenhof, on Oude Delft, is the **Museum Huis Lambert van Meerten,** which contains one of the country's most extensive collections of old Delft pottery and Dutch tiles.

If it's modern Delftware that interests you, you might like to tour the town's only surviving porcelain factory of some 30 which thrived in the 17th century. On weekdays, De Porceleyne Fles, a little off centre at Rotterdamseweg 196, welcomes visitors to view its showrooms and workshops. Another pottery, De Delftse Pauw, on Delftweg 133, is no less interesting.

Down the other end of Oude Delft, an arsenal dating from 1692 (Armamentarium) houses the Army Museum (Legermuseum).

What to Do

Shopping

Amsterdam has no prestigious shopping street like New York's Fifth Avenue, or London's Bond Street, but hundreds of small shops are scattered throughout the compact central area, offering everything from antique Delftware to rare Eastern spices.

There are also several open-

Boutiques and small shops make shopping a delight in Amsterdam.

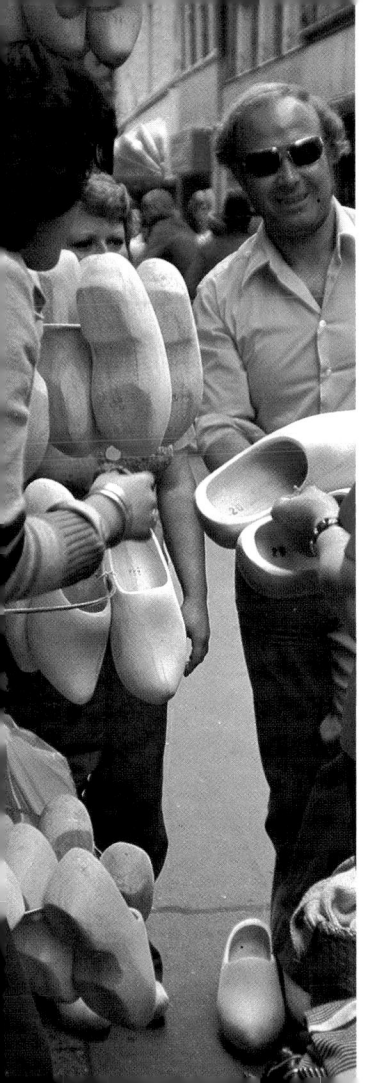

air markets. The best known is the flea-market (see p. 48), but also well worth a visit is the colourful, jostling, down-to-earth Albert Cuyp Market just south of the centre on tram routes 4, 7, 16, 24 and 25.

Shopping Hours

Most shops are open from 9 a.m. to 5.30 or 6 p.m., Monday to Saturday (though many of them don't open on Mondays till 1 p.m.). Some are open till 9 p.m. on Thursdays. English is widely spoken in shops.

What to Buy

Diamonds are top of the shopping list for many visitors to Amsterdam. The city has a well-earned, 400-year reputation for cutting and polishing, and the vast majority of merchants are thoroughly reliable. Notices all over town invite you to visit diamond exhibitions and tour workshops (there's no obligation to buy, of course). Taxi drivers are also well primed to whisk you

Wooden shoes make whimsical gifts. Amsterdam is rich in antiques but real bargains are scarce.

to their favourite diamond merchant if they hear a mention of the word.

Silver is another guaranteed buy, quality-controlled by government inspectors. (Gold cannot be called such unless it is at least 14-carat.)

Pewter has a long tradition in Holland. The painter Jan

day—if you've the money to spare. Amsterdam has 140 antique shops, a good 50 of them in Nieuwe Spiegelstraat and its extension near the Rijksmuseum. But remember that 50 per cent or so of the items on sale in the Spiegelstraat are said to come from Britain or France.

Vermeer was perhaps its first publicist in his 17th-century masterpieces. It's decorative as well as useful, and you can buy anything from a Dutch pewter ashtray, for just a few guilders, to an expensive traditional pot-bellied kettle.

Antiques are available in profusion. You'll have a field

Delft is another word synonymous with Holland, and the distinctive Dutch pottery is widely on sale in Amsterdam. Beware of imitations, and seek out a well-established store or an obviously expert dealer if you intend to spend heavily on it.

Makkum pottery is more **85**

delicate in colour and design than Delft and preferred by many local people. The genuine article is hand-painted and has the word Makkum on every piece.

Dutch cigars are world-famous, plentiful and cheap —an excellent purchase (see also p. 107).

Dutch gin *(jenever)* has a special taste. Made with juniper berries, it's fruitier and less fiery than English gin (see also p. 98).

If you are travelling by air, your best plan is to wait and do your liquor and tobacco shopping at Schiphol airport's much-vaunted tax-free shops.

Flowers and **plants** are of exceptional quality and variety—if you can carry them home and there are no import restrictions at the other end. Shopkeepers know all about mailing bulbs, if that's an alternative.

Souvenirs

For a more memorable holiday souvenir than the ubiquitous, mass-produced, miniature wooden shoes and windmills, try the old Jordaan area of town (see pp. 38–41). It has gained a reputation for in-shopping only in the last few years, and has no defined pattern. But seek, and you will

86

The Tile Standard

Antique dealers in Amsterdam say that the tile standard has taken over from the gold standard. The rarest ones can cost a small fortune nowadays—and the collector is just as likely to find them in a lowly farm-house as in some palatial mansion.

Since the first Dutch tiles were made in the 17th century, housewives of all ranks have liked to line their kitchens with them, for they are clean, durable, and highly attractive.

Modern tiles, it's agreed, are a poor substitute. They are thinner, and altogether too exact in design and glaze.

The really old tiles are often distinguished by the type of mortar clinging to them, by their thickness, and by the genuine quality of the design and glaze. Old bird motif tiles are rare and expensive, for example, and ships with three masts are collector's items, especially if they have a three-coloured flag.

Traditional Dutch tile production stopped about a century ago, but Spiegelstraat dealers still manage to find them around the countryside. Prices are highly variable.

find all sorts of off-beat little shops along the narrow streets, some in cellars, all within a few hundred yards of the Westerkerk landmark. Old, misshapen bottles, tea and exotic spices, beads, candles in 5,000 different shapes and sizes, rattan and bamboo basketwork and lampshades—these are just some of the fascinating items you'll find in the Jordaan shops.

Fancy dress is the order of the day on merry-making occasions.

Relaxing

You can skate, dance, go to a concert, ride a bike—the possibilities of relaxing in and around Amsterdam are varied and there is something to suit most tastes (you don't *really* want to ski, do you?).

Nightclubs in Amsterdam are only rarely of international standard. Around Rembrandtsplein in particular you will meet Holland's nearest approach to an out-and-out clip joint.

Discos are plentiful, especially around Leidseplein, but also scattered about the city and in some plush hotels.

Entry to discos and clubs is usually free—you'll simply pay more for drinks, according to what is being offered in entertainment and atmosphere. It's customary to tip the cloakroom (hat-check) attendant and the doorman.

Casino: The Casino Amsterdam in the Hilton Hotel offers roulette, blackjack and the like.

Cinemas are concentrated around Rembrandtsplein and Leidseplein. Everywhere, films are shown in the original language with Dutch sub-titles.

Music: The Concertgebouw Orchestra in the Concertgebouw itself (*gebouw* means building) is a musical treat—though tickets can be hard to obtain. The Netherlands Opera appears at the modern Stopera, in Waterlooplein (see p. 47).

Jazz: Weekends in the Joseph Lam Jazzclub, van Diemenstraat 8, and evenings (except Sundays) in the Bamboo Bar, Lange Leidsedwarsstraat 64. Also at Bimhuis, Oude Schans 73–77, and The String, Nes 98.

Ballet: Try to see the Dutch National Ballet in a classic—the "Stopera" is the venue—or the avant-garde Nederlands Danstheater, much acclaimed in recent years.

Marionettes: The Komedie van Hout (Comedy of Wood) takes the music of Mozart as its inspiration. An ensemble of puppeteers ambitiously stage his magical operas.

The **Holland Festival** of art, music, dance and theatre takes place throughout the country, but mainly in Amsterdam, each June. Tickets to attend star events can be difficult to obtain, unless you apply well in advance.

Artis Zoo in Plantage Middenlaan (tram 9) has a wonderfully informal atmosphere. Founded in 1838, it has the usual range—from elephants to mice—but with specially strong sections of tropical birds, plus a children's farm where all kinds of domestic and barnyard animals can be touched and tended.

The **Botanical Gardens** *(Hortus Botanicus)* are within walking distance of Rembrandtsplein (or tram 9).

Dam Square and Vondel Park may be the venues for special events.

Festivals in Amsterdam

February
Just before Lent, there's a limited spillover from southern Holland's Carnival excesses in some Amsterdam bars and streets: fancy dress, dancing, a larger-than-usual consumption of beer and a non-stop oompah-pah of Dutch music.

March
The Amsterdam Art Weeks Festival offers a wide variety of cultural activities such as opera, dance, ballet, theatre (including English-speaking companies) and exhibitions.

April
April 30 is called Queen's Day, a public holiday when everyone turns out. Children set up stalls, selling anything from home-made cake to broken toys. Street musicians are allowed to busk for the day and collect money. Portrait-sketchers flourish, and food stalls appear everywhere. A unique local celebration you should try not to miss.

June–July
The Holland Festival is a more up-market cultural occasion of music, opera, ballet, theatre and recitals. Plan well in advance if you want tickets for the more popular events, which take place in the country's larger cities, though mainly in Amsterdam.

This festival is paralleled by the Vondelpark Festival. From Wednesday to Sunday there are free open-air performances of music, dance and theatre, and children's plays.

August
Uitmarkt, last weekend in August, marks the beginning of the new season. Thousands of people are attracted to the free music and theatre performances.

September
At the beginning of the month, a huge floral parade wends its way from Aalsmeer to Amsterdam and back.

The second Friday in the month sees the start of the Jordaan Festival, ten days of fun and frolic in this friendliest part of the old city.

November–December
In the middle of November, Holland's St. Nicolaus (or Sinterklaas) arrives by boat from Spain with his Moorish servant, Black Pete, and tours town on a white horse. December 5 heralds *pakjesavond* (Parcels Night), a traditional family festival. The next day, Sinterklaas leaves for Spain again.

Skating on frozen canal to celebrate arrival of unusually cold winter.

Sports

There's water, water everywhere, thus many water sports are at hand. So great, in fact, is the demand for **boats and yachts** on the lakes near the city that it's practically impossible to hire a vessel at short notice during the summer. As to Amsterdam's canals, you can take advantage of them by hiring water bicycles, motorboats or small houseboats (including skipper). But equally, book early.

You can **water-ski** at some lakes and **swim** from the miles of sandy North Sea beaches (remembering that the water is at Northern European temperatures).

For **skating,** there's the Jaap Eden stadium, with both indoor and outdoor rinks, on Radioweg (tram 9; buses 8, 59). The Dutch are high among the world-champion speed skaters, and in winter you could watch a big race here, or an international ice-hockey match. Sad to say, even in the depths of winter you are unlikely to witness throngs of **91** skaters on the canals, whatever those old paintings may have led you to expect. Nowadays, it's rarely cold enough for the waterways to freeze over.

Off the water, **soccer** is the Dutch sporting passion. With the right contacts you could get a ticket to see Amsterdam's idolized Ajax (pronounced EYE-ax) in action.

Cycling is a favourite means of getting about in both town and country. For a pleasure ride, pick a Sunday if you can, when the traffic is thinnest. Holland's flatness is a distinct advantage—if the wind isn't against you (see also pp. 105–106).

More than 30 **tennis** courts are for hire at the Tenniscentrum "Nieuw BV" at Lotsylaan 8 (bus 26 from Leidseplein, tram 5). For other tennis, and also **squash**, facilities, contact the VVV, tel. 26 64 44.

For **horse-riding**, try the Amsterdamse Bos (Amsterdam Woods). Stables here rent out mounts for group rides (bus 26).

Golfers are less catered for. Unless you can contrive an introduction to the Amsterdam Golf Club at Duivendrecht, you may be reduced to doing a circuit of **mini-golf** in Sloterpark (President Allendelaan).

Wining and Dining

The claim is made that Amsterdam offers more variety in food and restaurants than any other European city—London included. Indisputably, pride of place goes to Indonesian cuisine, well ahead of the native Dutch in popularity. Thanks to the influence of three centuries of colonial presence in the Far East, in most of the country's major towns, at least, you are more likely to eat Indonesian than traditional Dutch.

Restaurants
While Indonesian and Chinese restaurants are the most numerous within Amsterdam's compact city centre, the remarkable international list also takes in Surinamese, Yugoslavian, Spanish, Scandinavian, Japanese, Greek, Hungarian, French, Italian, Pakistani, and Turkish (with belly-dancers) as well as several macrobiotic establishments.

Can you eat Dutch, too? Strangely, true local cuisine is hard to find, though 170 proprietors claim to serve it. A few of them advertise *Dutch restaurant,* in English, on the door.

Fit for a rajah, rijsttafel *spread is succulent, spicy and immense.*

There are about 40 restaurants in town that offer a "tourist menu". This sign, accompanied by a fork motif, proclaims the availability of a set-price, three-course meal. This is generally good, simple fare, and excellent value for money.

Most menus are printed in two or three languages, almost always including English (though occasionally it will be in French only).

All taxes and service charges will be included in your bill, but it's customary to round off payment or give an extra guilder or two if the service has been particularly good.

Amsterdam restaurants are as varied in atmosphere as in menu. You can dine with a top-floor view over the city or in a cellar at canal water level, in a windmill or a former church, or anywhere in between.

So: here's to good eating in Amsterdam, or *eet smakelijk,* as the Dutch say.*

---

* The Berlitz EUROPEAN MENU READER includes an extensive glossary of Dutch (and Indonesian) food with English equivalents in a handy, pocket-sized reference book.

Eating Indonesian Style

Let's start off with what the Dutch have come to regard as their national dish, the almost mandatory Indonesian *rijsttafel* (literally, rice-table).

There are up to 32 items in a *rijsttafel*. When this overwhelming array arrives at your table, together with rice and a large soup bowl, tackle the feast this way: put a mound of rice in the centre of your plate, and build around the edges of the mound with spoonfuls from your dishes of *babi ketjap* (pork in soya sauce), *daging bronkos* (roast meat in coconut-milk sauce), *sambal goreng kering* (spicy pimiento and fish paste), *oblo-oblo* (mixed soya beans) etc.

Anything containing the word *sambal* will be peppery-hot, especially the tiny portions of *sambal* that look like a ketchup paste but have been aptly described by waiters as "explosion, Sir!"

Even the dish of mixed fruit in syrup, *rudjak manis*, will be spicy hot. All in all, what with the crisp, puffy shrimp bread, sour cucumber, cut-up chicken, the nuts, the fried banana—not forgetting the skewers of cubed meat with peanut sauce called *sateh*—the rice-table is an unforgettable eating experience.

If you can't tackle the full *rijsttafel*, you might like to try the smaller and cheaper *nasi goreng*, commonly called a *mini-rijsttafel*, a single serving on a plate. A *nasi goreng* will cost about one-half the price of a *rijsttafel*, depending on size and restaurant.

Going Dutch

Most non-specialist restaurants offer a mélange of international cooking—*entrecôtes*, schnitzels, spaghetti dishes etc.—with just a few distinctive Dutch twists. *Biefstuk* for example, is a steak, but always pan-fried, not grilled. Home-fried potatoes, in the Dutch version, are often fried whole, not sliced.

Holland's famous pea soup (*erwtensoep*, pronounced AIR-te-soop) is rich and thick, a small meal in itself. This, or the other native soup speciality, *bruine bonensoep* (red kidney-bean soup), will often be found on the menu of traditional Dutch restaurants along with the country's variety of winter-warming potato hashes headed by *hutspot*, a mix of potatoes, carrots and onions, sometimes supplemented with *klapstuk* (beef). *Stamppot* is the generic name for potato and vegetable hashes, which are often hollowed on top to make room for a fat Dutch sausage *(worst)*. *Boerenkool* is the most famous *stamppot,* the vegetable this time being curly kale.

Fish in Amsterdam is fresh and excellent. Sole *(tong)* is plentiful, and served in a dozen classically French ways: with fruit, with shrimp, with mushrooms, with wine sauce—even just poached or grilled on its own. There's also good fresh salmon *(zalm),* halibut *(heilbot),* turbot *(tarbot),* cod *(kabeljauw),* haddock *(schelvis)* as well as local oysters *(oesters)* and mussels *(mosselen)*. Smoked eel *(ge-*

rookte paling) is a Dutch delight you just shouldn't miss.

If Dutch meat tends to vary widely in quality, local vegetables are first-class. Artichoke *(artisjokken)* in season is a readily available starter, and for the main course there's a full range of peas *(erwtjes),* beans *(bonen),* spinach *(spinazie),* carrots *(worteltjes)* and brussels sprouts *(spruitjes)* etc. An agreeable Dutch habit from colonial days is to sprinkle nutmeg on the greens.

Salads are good, but limited

Snack stand specializes in smoked eel. Dutch enjoy raw herring, too.

in style—a routine presentation of lettuce, tomato, green peppers and raw onion liberally doused in an oil and vinegar dressing. They are usually served with the meal. For a salad starter you can get "Russian egg" *(russisch ei)*, a hard-boiled egg with fish and raw vegetables, or "hussars' salad" *(huzarenslaatje)*, a creamy mix of potato, raw vegetables and meat.

There's no tradition in Holland of taking cheese after the main course. The Dutch prefer their Edam, Gouda and Leidsekaas (Leiden cheese) for lunch and breakfast.

The Dutch are not great dessert-eaters, but that's no reason for you to follow suit. Dutch apple tart *(appeltaart)* is usually available, with its filling of apples, sultanas and cinnamon. So is fresh fruit. *Flensjes* are thin pancakes. And if you like a spicy-cool dessert, try the typically Dutch *gember met slagroom* (lumps of fresh ginger with lots of cream).

Breakfast *(ontbijt)*
With such a hearty meal, it's no wonder the Dutch still can't tackle a dessert after dinner. Three of four kinds of bread are mandatory, including currant bread and a rye bread,

plus ham, plus sliced cheese, plus jam, plus the question, "And would you like an egg, Sir?" Paradoxically, the larger hotels these days charge you extra for a smaller breakfast, whereas the small family hotels will give you this formidable feast with the price of the room.

Snacks

Here, the well-known Dutch sandwich shops (broodjeswinkels) come into their own.

The sandwich takes the form of a soft bread roll stuffed with maybe five or six slices of ham, cheese or liversausage, or with overflowing spoonfuls of shrimp, creamed salad or tartar meat.

Broodjeswinkels are fast on service, appear to be everopen, and always display the price list prominently.

Another Dutch tradition is pancakes (pannekoeken). On Sunday afternoons particularly, you'll see whole families popping out for pancakes. They're a really substantial snack, offered in a wide range. Some have apple rings cooked in with them, others include

currants, ginger, bacon or cheese. You can get them plain, too. If you have a particularly sweet tooth, smother them in sugar or molasses (stroop) as the Dutch usually do.

Beverages

All Dutch restaurants are licensed to serve beer, wine and spirits.

All wine is imported (there is a wide range of French and German vintages on

Functional sandwich shops, cosy bars belong to Dutch way of life.

most lists). If you want to economize, ask for open wine *(open wijn)*.

Along with coffee—perhaps second to it—beer *(pils)* is the national drink, served normally from the tap. It's a deliciously consistent, light-coloured lager, stronger than standard British or American beer, and is cooled to a constant temperature of 45–46 °F (7–8 °C). The standard Dutch beer glass holds only a third of a pint.

Dutch brandy *(vieux)* is half the price of cognac and milder. *Jenever* is a juniper-flavoured drink along the lines of English gin but less strong. It is served chilled in special small glasses, topped almost to overflowing, and is best drunk without tonic, orange juice or any other admixture. There are the clear *jonge* (young) *jenevers*, and the *oude* (old), which are more mature and yellowish. Inquisitive strangers are advised to test the *jonge* to begin with. More palatable, perhaps, for beginners are special *jenevers* such as *bessen* (blackcurrant) or *citroen* (lemon).

Coffee *(koffie)*, the national drink, must be freshly made, or the Dutch will send it back to the kitchen. It's usually served black, but you'll be offered cream in the form of Dutch *koffiemelk,* a thick evaporated variety which should be used sparingly if you want to retain any taste in your coffee.

Tea *(thee)* is usually served in tea-bag form with lemon.

Bars and Cafés

Amsterdam's bars and cafés open at all sorts of hours, but the general pattern is from mid-morning till 1 a.m., extending to 2 a.m. on Fridays and Saturdays.

Children are allowed into Dutch bars, and you don't have to be a regular to feel at ease.

The most authentic are undoubtedly the city's *bruine cafés,* so called because they're usually dark-wood panelled and nicotine-stained. You'll find these throughout the old city centre, with the best examples towards, and in, the Jordaan district, where idiosyncrasies abound. There are bars here where working-class locals sing grand opera on a Sunday afternoon, accompanied by a lone accordionist; bars for students or fashion models; bars where a museum curator rubs shoulders with a flea-market stallholder; and one selling 60 different beers.

To help you order...

Could we have a table?	**Heeft u een tafel voor ons?**			
Do you have a set menu?	**Heeft u een vast menu?**			
I'd like a/an/some...	**Ik zou graag...willen hebben.**			

beer	**een pils**	napkin	**een servet**
bread	**een brood**	pepper	**de peper**
coffee	**koffie**	potatoes	**aardappelen**
cutlery	**een bestek**	rice	**rijst**
dessert	**dessert**	salad	**sla**
fish	**vis**	salt	**het zout**
glass	**een glas**	soup	**soep**
ice-cream	**ijs**	sugar	**de suiker**
meat	**vlees**	tea	**thee**
menu	**een menu**	vegetables	**groente(n)**
milk	**melk**	(iced) water	**(ijs)water**
mustard	**mosterd**	wine	**wijn**

...and read the menu

aardappelpuree	mashed potatoes	**meloen**	melon (cantaloupe)
aardbeien	strawberries		
abrikoos	apricot	**niertje**	kidney
ananas	pineapple	**paprika**	green peppers
belegd broodje	sandwich roll	**patates frites**	chips (US French fries)
biefstuk	steak		
bloemkool	cauliflower	**perzik**	peach
citroen	lemon	**pruimen**	plums
ei(eren)	egg(s)	**rundvlees**	beef
forel	trout	**sinaasappel**	orange
frambozen	raspberries	**sla**	lettuce; salad
garnalen	shrimp, prawns	**sperciebonen**	French beans
kaas	cheese	**uien**	onions
kalfsvlees	veal	**uitsmijter**	ham, roast beef or cheese and eggs on bread
karbonade	chop		
kersen	cherries		
kip	chicken	**varkensvlees**	pork
konijn	rabbit	**verse paling**	fresh eel
kool	cabbage	**warme**	hot
lamsvlees	lamb	**gehaktbal**	meatball
lever(worst)	liver (sausage)	**worstje**	sausage

99

BY SEA

Train-Boat-Train: The favourite route from Britain is via Harwich and the Hook of Holland, with departures every day. If you're not much of a sailor, you might prefer the shorter sea route across the Channel to Belgium or France with a longer train ride north.

Car ferries: Travellers leaving from the south of England will find the Harwich–Hook of Holland crossing the most convenient. Those visitors coming from the North and Scotland might prefer the Hull–Rotterdam service.

Bus-Boat-Bus: Certain British bus companies operate cheap regular services between London's Victoria Coach Station and Amsterdam.

BY RAIL

Visitors from outside Europe who intend to do a lot of rail travelling around continental Europe may be interested in purchasing a *Eurailpass*. This flat-rate, unlimited-mileage ticket is valid for first-class travel practically anywhere in western Europe except Great Britain. Visitors under 26 can get the second-class Eurail Youthpass. These tickets must be bought before you leave home.

The *Rail Europ Senior* card, obtainable before departure only, entitles senior citizens (60+) to purchase train tickets for European destinations at reduced prices.

Any family of at least 3 people can buy a *Rail-Europe F* (family) card: the holder pays full price, the rest of the family obtain a 50% reduction in the Netherlands and 14 other European contries; the whole family is also entitled to a 30% reduction on Sealink and Hoverspeed Channel crossings.

Anyone under 26 years of age can purchase an *Interrail* card which allows one month's unlimited 2nd-class travel in some 20 European countries. The Holland Rail Pass, obtainable at any railway station in Holland, entitles the holder to three days' unlimited train travel within a period of 15 days and to discounts on special excursions offered by Netherlands Railways. Up to three children aged between 4 and 11 accompanying the holder (who should be over 18) travel at only *f* 3 each.

When to Go

Holland's climate is as unpredictable as Britain's. Summer days can be either rainy and chilly or gloriously hot and dry—or both alternately. In winter, icy-cold weather rarely prevails for more than a few days at a time. It's more often rainy. Spring and autumn are characterized by cooler, equally unstable weather, though mild—even warm—spells are by no means uncommon.

		J	F	M	A	M	J	J	A	S	O	N	D
Temperature	°F	39	39	42	51	57	61	67	65	57	51	42	39
	°C	4	4	6	10	14	16	19	18	14	10	6	4

Figures shown are approximate monthly averages.

Planning Your Budget

To give you an idea of what to expect, here's a list of average prices in Dutch guilders *(f)*. They can only be *approximate,* however, as inflation creeps relentlessly up.

Airport transfer. Train airport–Central Station *f*4.40, taxi *f*45.·

Babysitters. *f*4 per hour up to midnight, *f*5 thereafter, *f*5.50 during daytime.

Bicycle rental. *f*7 per day, deposit *f*50–200.

Buses and trams. 3-strip ticket *f*2.70, 10-strip ticket *f*9, 15-strip ticket *f*9.05. Day ticket for all public transport *f*9.

Camping (per night). *f*8 per person, all in, *f*6 per car, *f*3–6 per tent, children under 9 free.

Canal tours. *f*9–12 for one hour, "candlelight tour" *f*30–40.

Car rental. *Ford Fiesta 1100 CL f*68 per day, *f*0.68 per kilometre, *f*966 per week with unlimited mileage. *Ford Sierra 1600 L f*98 per day, *f*0.98 per kilometre, *f*1,306 per week with unlimited mileage. *BMW 316 f*188 per day, *f*1.88 per km., *f*2,576 per week with unlimited mileage. Add 18.5% tax.

Cigarettes. *f*4.25 for a packet of 25, *f*8 for a packet of 20 cigarillos, *f*5.50 for 5 medium-sized cigars.

Guides (personal). *f*170 for half-day, *f*275 for full day.

Hairdressers. Shampoo and set *f*45, permanent wave *f*100, manicure *f*20. **Barbers:** haircut *f*15–25.

Hotels (double room with bath). Luxury *f*350–500, 1st class *f*200–350, medium *f*125–200, moderate *f*85–125 (with shower). Boarding house *f*40–85. B+B *f*17.50–50. Youth hostel *f*18.50 (members), *f*23.50 (non members).

Meals and drinks. Lunch *f*10–25, dinner *f*25–55, coffee *f*2, *jenever* *f*3, gin and tonic *f*10, beer *f*2.25, soft drink *f*2.25, sandwich *f*2.50.

Metro. 2 zones *f*2.70. Day ticket for all public transport *f*9.

Museum ticket (one year; passport photo required). Up to age 25 *f*15, over age 25 *f*40, senior citizens *f*25.

An A–Z Summary of Practical Information and Facts

Listed after most main entries is an appropriate Dutch translation, usually in the singular.

AIRPORT *(luchthaven)*. Schiphol, 15 kilometres south-west of Amsterdam, is a showpiece modern airport, with moving walkways, conference rooms, snack-bars, a hotel information desk, currency exchange services, a post office, car rental counters, a children's nursery, a barber's shop and ladies' hairdresser, extensive tax-free shops, etc. Porters *(kruier)* are scarce, but free baggage trolleys are plentiful.

Every 15 minutes a KLM-hotel bus leaves for the major hotels in Amsterdam. A train leaves every 30 minutes for Amsterdam Central Station, with direct connections to towns all over Holland. The journey from the airport takes about 15 minutes. For flights with KLM or with an airline for which KLM handles the formalities, passengers can check in at the KLM desk in the Amsterdam, Rotterdam or The Hague central railway station. Taxis are always available, metered, and with tips included.

The Dutch Railways also operate a half-hourly train service from Amsterdam RAI (Congress Centre) to Schiphol, a ten-minute ride.

BABYSITTERS *(babysit or oppas)*. If your hotel can't find a baby-sitter for you, try the VVV tourist-information office, which has a list of bilingual sitters.

Can you get us a babysitter for tonight?

Kunt u ons voor vanavond een babysit bezorgen?

BICYCLE and MOPED RENTAL *(fietsverhuur; bromfietsverhuur)*. Though most Amsterdammers own a bicycle, there are many rental agencies, one of them at Central Station (24 83 91). All are listed in the Yellow Pages. You have to pay a substantial deposit.

The cyclist is so much a part of Dutch life that all modern roads include a cycle path. On these paths there are special traffic signs, showing a cycle symbol. In all cases, the cyclist is regarded as a first-

B class citizen, and has to be treated with respect by the motorist (see also DRIVING IN HOLLAND). Unfortunately, veterans of the Amsterdam cycle paths don't always show the same respect for fellow riders. If you aren't used to a bike, be careful—Dutch cyclists don't bother too much with traffic rules.

C **CAMPING** *(camping)*. The Netherlands as a whole is well provided with campsites. The sites are usually clean and have full facilities. It's best to book in advance.

Have you room for a tent/ a caravan (trailer)?	**Heeft u plaats voor een tent/ caravan?**

CANAL TOURS *(grachtenrondvaart)*. Boats provide interesting tours of the major canals, complete with guide, or at least multilingual tape-recorded commentary on the sights. There are many pick-up points in the city centre.

You can choose from all kinds of tours, ranging from the one-hour canal tour to the super "candlelight tour" with wine and buffet included.

You can also hire your own sailingboat (including skipper), a motor-boat or a water bicycle.

The Canalbus is a boat that leaves every 30 minutes between 10 a.m. and 8 p.m. from Central Station and stops at Leidsestraat, Rijks-museum, Leidseplein and Westerkerk.

CAR RENTAL *(autoverhuur)*. Everything under the sun is on offer. All the major international agencies are represented in Amsterdam, and more than 40 others are listed in the Yellow Pages under *Autoverhuur*. There are several car rental counters at Schiphol airport.

Conditions of hire are usually strictly adhered to. You'll need a valid national or international driving licence, held for at least 12 months. The driver must be at least 21 years of age, and 23 for some firms. It's advisable to take your passport along to the agency, too.

I'd like to hire a car.	**Ik zou graag een auto willen huren.**
today/tomorrow	**vandaag/morgen**
for one day/a week	**voor één dag/één week**
Please include full insurance.	**Met een all-risk verzekering alstublieft.**

CIGARETTES, CIGARS, TOBACCO *(sigaretten; sigaren; tabak).*
Cigarettes are usually sold in packets of 25. A full range of both local and international makes are available at tobacconists' *(sigarenhandelaar)* and from vending machines. Hotels and restaurants also sell them. A lot of Dutch people roll their own cigarettes *(shag).*

The world-famed Dutch cigars, which are not at all expensive, range from mini cigarillos through medium-sized (and sometimes handmade) varieties to torpedoes of Churchillian proportions. Renowned for their aroma, they use pure Indonesian, particularly Sumatran, tobacco with no additives—a legacy from the colonial days when Amsterdam was the world's biggest tobacco market.

Pipe tobacco, from the many famous Dutch manufacturers, is also plentiful.

A packet of cigarettes/A box of matches, please.	**Een pakje sigaretten/Een doosje lucifers, alstublieft.**

CLOTHING *(kleding).* Informality is the keynote during the daytime. In the evening, at the better restaurants and hotels, men are required to wear a jacket (though not necessarily a tie), and women would not be out of place in a cocktail dress. In summer, unless you happen to hit upon a really exceptional heatwave, a light sweater or wrap may be needed in the evenings. Spring and autumn only rarely produce balmy days—let alone evenings—and the only sensible way to dress in winter is to bundle up well, for the wind can be piercing—or exhilarating, if you look at it like that. Always pack a raincoat, light or heavy according to season: even during a fine, hot summer, brief showers are possible. Comfortable walking shoes are essential, in all seasons, and maybe rubber overshoes in all but summer. On the beaches, anything goes—or comes off. Topless bathing is general practice in the open air, and some well-marked naturist beaches are to be found all along the North Sea coast.

Wil I need a jacket and tie?	**Moet ik een jasje en een das aan?**
Is it all right if I wear this?	**Kan ik dit dragen?**

COMMUNICATIONS

Post Office *(postkantoor):* There are two main post offices and many district offices around town. The head office *(hoofdpostkantoor)* is at Singel 250, at the corner with Raadhuisstraat, just beyond the Royal Palace on Dam Square) and the other main office is a Ooster-

C dokskade 3–5 (a little off the beaten track, just east of Central Station). See also HOURS. When buying postcards from stands and souvenir shops, you can usually get the appropriate stamps *(postzegel)* on the spot. Dutch boxes are red and have two slots, in Amsterdam marked AMSTERDAM and OVERIGE BESTEMMINGEN (other destinations).

Mail *(post):* For longer stays (if you don't know your address beforehand) you can have your mail sent *poste restante* (general delivery) to one of the main post offices mentioned above. Don't forget that identification is necessary when picking up your mail.

Telegram *(telegram):* The easiest way to send a cable is to ask your hotel porter or switchboard to send it for you. Otherwise, you can dial 009 yourself, where the operator will deal efficiently with it. To avoid the slightest chance of an important word being wrongly transmitted, go yourself to the head post office at Singel 250 for 24-hour cable service.

Telephone *(telefoon):* You can dial direct from Amsterdam to almost all of Europe, including Britain and Eire, and to the U.S.A., Canada and South Africa. At Telehouse, Raadhuisstraat 46–50, behind Dam Square, there's a 24-hour service for international calls.

For some services, you'll have to go through the operator. To make a personal (person-to-person) call, if you want to air your Dutch specify *ik wil een gesprek met voorbericht;* for a transferred-charge (collect) call, say *ik wil telefoneren op kosten van de ontvanger.*

inland enquiries	008
international enquiries	06-0418
alternatively, for all calls	06-0410

CONSULATES *(consulaat).* Most countries have a consulate in Amsterdam; the majority of embassies are in The Hague. A complete list can be found in the Yellow Pages under "Ambassades/consulaten".

Australia: Koninginnegracht 23–24, The Hague; tel. (070) 364 79 08

Canada: Sophialaan 7, The Hague; tel. (070) 361 41 11

Eire: Dr. Kuyperstraat 9, The Hague; tel. (070) 363 09 93

Great Britain: Koningslaan 44, Amsterdam; tel. (020) 76 43 43

108 New Zealand: Mauritskade 25, The Hague; tel. (070) 346 93 24

South Africa: Wassenaarseweg 36, The Hague; tel. (070) 392 45 01
U.S.A.: Museumplein 19, Amsterdam; tel. (020) 64 56 61 and 79 03 21

Where's the… consulate?	**Waar is het… consulaat?**
American/Australian/British	**Amerikaanse/Australische/Britse**
Canadian/Irish/New Zealand	**Canadese/Ierse/Nieuwzeelandse**
South African	**Zuidafrikaanse**

CONVERTER CHARTS. For fluid and distance measures, see page 112. Holland uses the metric system.

Temperature

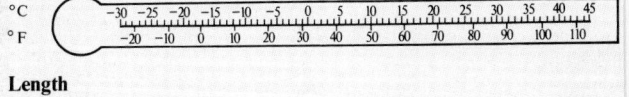

Length

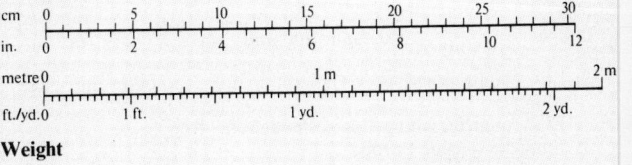

Weight

CRIME and THEFT *(misdrijf; diefstal).* Unfortunately, petty crime and stealing are widespread in Amsterdam. In what was once the most innocent of capital cities, even the department stores now display warnings in several languages urging customers to beware of pickpockets. If you do lose your wallet of handbag, report the loss to the nearest police station. Be careful around the red-light district and off the main entertainment squares. It's better to take a taxi home than to walk through the back streets or go for a stroll in the Vondel Park after dark.

I want to report a theft.	**Ik wil aangifte doen van een diefstal.**

C **CUSTOMS FORMALITIES** *(douaneformaliteiten)*. See also Driving
in Holland. The following chart shows what main duty-free items
you may take into Holland and, when returning home, into your own
country:

Entering the Netherlands from:	Cigarettes		Cigars		Tobacco	Spirits	Wine
1)	200	or	50	or	250 g.	1 l. and 2 l.	
2)	300	or	75	or	400 g.	1.5 l. and 5 l.	
3)	400	or	100	or	500 g.	1 l. and 2 l.	
Into:							
Canada	200	and	50	and	900 g.	1.1 l. or 1.1 l.	
Eire	200	or	50	or	250 g.	1 l. and 2 l.	
U.K.	200	or	50	or	250 g.	1 l. and 2 l.	
U.S.A.	200	and	100	and	4)	1 l. or 1 l.	

1) EEC countries with goods bought tax free, and other European
   countries
2) EEC countries with goods not bought tax free
3) countries outside Europe
4) a reasonable quantity

Most visitors, including British, American, Canadian and Irish, need
only a valid passport—no visa—to enter the Netherlands. (British
subjects can even enter on the simplified Visitor's Passport.) Though
European and North American residents are not subject to any health
requirements, visitors from further afield may require a smallpox vac-
cination. Check with your travel agent before departure.

Currency restrictions: From the Dutch side, there are no limits on
import or export. But check on your own country's possible restrictions.

I've nothing to declare.	**Ik heb niets aan te geven.**
It's for my personal use.	**Het is voor eigen gebruik.**

Entering Holland: To take your car into Holland you will require:

Valid national or international driving licence	Green Card—an extension to your regular insurance policy making it valid for travel abroad (Green Card regulations between European countries, especially within the EEC, are constantly being relaxed, so check with your own insurance when planning your trip).
Car registration papers	
National identity sticker on back of car	
Red warning triangle for use in case of breakdown	

Driving conditions: Drive on the right, pass on the left. Generally, traffic coming from your right has priority. On motorways (expressways), this rule applies only at roundabouts uncontrolled by lights. On other main roads, internationally standardized signs will give you clear right of way over the side roads.

But beware at all times in cities, and especially on the Amsterdam canals—many Dutch drivers have an ingrained habit of darting out from the right. At every junction on the canals, reduce speed to less than walking pace to avoid the danger or being hit from the right.

Beware again, in Amsterdam and other cities, of cyclists. At night, many of them ride along almost invisibly, without lights. At all times, remember that you must not cut across them when turning right. Check in your mirror constantly. Be careful also when getting out of your car, in case a bicycle runs into the open door.

Trams have priority over everything on wheels or legs. Give way to them in any circumstances. Buses leaving from bus stops also have priority.

Motor-cycle, moped and scooter drivers and passengers must wear crash helmets. If a foreign car has seat belts, they must be worn.

Speed limits are well signposted: 30 or 50 kilometres per hour (kph) in built-up areas, 100 or 120 kph on motorways and generally 80 kph on other roads.

Parking: It needs patience, but can be done. There are very few large public car parks compared with other cities, for the centre of Amsterdam is still a densely built, 17th-century town. Parking is possible along the canalsides, however, with most stretches metered and some not. Meters take ƒ2.50, ƒ1 or 25-cent coins. In the centre you will need a lot. Traffic police are very vigilant. Being even a few minutes late **111**

D could mean a wheel clamp or having your car towed away by traffic police. Either measure will cost you a lot of money.

Drinking and driving: These two activities are virtually incompatible in Holland: with more than 0.5 millilitres of alcohol in your system per litre of blood (at the most two beers or the equivalent) you may lose your driving licence and face a hefty fine.

Fuel and oil *(benzine; olie):* Service stations are plentiful and fuel prices fairly standard throughout Holland. Fuel is available in 95 octane lead-free *(Euro loodvrij),* 98 octane lead-free *(Super Plus),* 91 octane not lead-free *(Super)* and diesel. Some garages offer a few cents discount *(korting).* Most stations are self service. Oil is available in all standard grades.

Breakdowns: Emergency telephones line the motorways at regular intervals. If you're lucky enough to break down just next to a small yellow van bearing a sign *wegenwacht* (WW) on its roof, then the Dutch automobile association (ANWB) emergency service is on the spot. The WW's emergency number is 06-0888.

Fluid measures

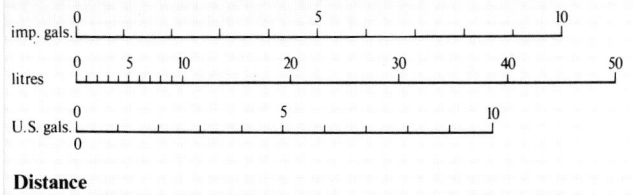

Distance

Road signs: International pictographs are in widespread use, but here are some written signs you may encounter:

Doorgaand verkeer	Through traffic	**Fietsers**	Cyclists
Eenrichtings-verkeer	One-way traffic	**Filevorming**	Bottleneck
		Gevaarlijke bocht	Dangerous bend
Einde inhaal-verbod	End of no-pass zone	**Inhaalverbod**	No overtaking (passing)

Let op...	Watch out for...	Tegenliggers	Oncoming traffic
Omleiding	Diversion (Detour)	**Uitrit**	Exit
Parkeerverbod	No parking	**Verboden in te rijden**	No entry for vehicles...
Pas op...	Attention	**Verkeer over één rijbaan**	Single-lane traffic
Rechts houden	Keep right		
Slecht wegdek	Bad road surface	**Voetgangers**	Pedestrians
		Wegomlegging	Diversion
Snelheid ver-minderen	Reduce speed	**Werk in uit-voering**	Roadworks in progress
Stoplichten op 100 m	Traffic lights at 100 metres	**Wielrijders**	Cyclists
		Zachte berm	Soft shoulders

(international) driving licence	**(internationaal) rijbewijs**
car registration papers	**kentekenbewijs**
green card	**groene kaart**
Are we on the right road for...?	**Is dit de goede weg naar...?**
Fill her up, please, with...	**Vol, graag, met...**
super	**super**
regular	**normaal**
Please check the oil/tyres/battery.	**Wilt u de olie/banden/accu controleren?**
I've had a breakdown.	**Ik heb autopech.**
There's been an accident.	**Er is een ongeluk gebeurd.**

DRUGS. If you've heard that Amsterdam is soft on drugs, beware. The possession of both soft and hard drugs is actually illegal, and there are penalties ranging from four to 12 years for drug offences. Police know well that hashish is smoked in certain bars and sub-culture clubs. But their attitude is getting tougher all the time towards dealers in hard *or* soft drugs.

ELECTRIC CURRENT *(elektriciteit)*. Everywhere, 220-volt, 50-cycle current is standard. Plugs and sockets are different from both British and American, but your hotel receptionist will usually have an adaptor to spare.

I'd like a plug adaptor/battery.	**Ik wil graag een verloopstekker/ een batterij.**

E **EMERGENCIES** *(noodgeval)*. Depending on the nature of the emergency, refer to the separate entries in this section such as CONSULATES, MEDICAL CARE, POLICE, etc. If there's no time, your hotel staff or a taxi driver will certainly help. Language is unlikely to be a problem.

Here are a few useful telephone numbers for urgent matters:

Police	22 22 22	Ambulance	5 55 55 55
Fire	21 21 21	ANWB (Dutch auto-mobile association)	06-0888

And a few words for the unexpected occasion:

Careful	**Pas op**	Help	**Hulp**
Danger	**Gevaar**	Police	**Politie**
Fire	**Brand**	Stop	**Halt**

G **GUIDES and INTERPRETERS** *(gids; tolk)*. Most city sightseeing and canal-boat tours will be accompanied by a multilingual guide. For business or private purposes contact Gidsencentrale, tel. (070) 320 25 45. Interpreters are listed in the Yellow Pages under 'Tolken'.

H **HAIRDRESSERS** *(kapper)*. Most of the major hotels have their own salons, but in any case the hotel receptionist will recommend a favourite place nearby. All barber shops and most beauty salons close on Tuesdays.

haircut	**knippen**
shampoo and set	**wassen en watergolven**
permanent wave	**permanenten**

HITCH-HIKING *(liften)*. A common practice in Holland is to hold a card or sign with your destination clearly written on it.

Can you give us a lift to...?	**Kunt u ons een lift geven naar...?**

HOLLAND LEISURE CARD. The card entitles non-residents to substantial discounts on car hire, public transport, domestic air travel, admission to many tourist attractions, as well as discounts on purchases at a leading department store and the Amsterdam Diamond Centre and free entry to casinos. The Holland Leisure Card is valid for one year. It can be purchased at NBT offices (see p. 123), selected VVV tourist offices. Dutch Railways (NS) travel agencies and Grenswissel-kantoren (at railway stations and border crossings).

HOTELS and ACCOMMODATION *(hotel; logies)*. See also CAMP-ING. The strong guilder of recent years has made Amsterdam accommodation seem expensive to travellers from weak-currency countries. Nevertheless, there's a wide range available, from luxury international palaces to small family canalside hotels. Single rooms are hard to find, especially at smaller hotels. During holiday periods, when the whole town seems to be brimming with out-of-town visitors, the VVV tourist-information office opposite the Central Station runs admirable booking services. They rarely fail to find a room, though it may well be beyond your intended price range. Moral: book in advance if possible at peak times.

Dutch tourist-information offices will give you a hotel list which incorporates both a quality assessment and a one- to five-star rating system. Off-season rates are reduced a little. In all but the luxury-class and many first-class hotels, breakfast is usually included in the room rate (but check beforehand). It will normally be a very copious Dutch breakfast (see p. 96), not just a light continental starter for the day.

Boarding houses *(pension),* not bookable through the VVV service, are even cheaper than a moderate hotel.

For the motorist there are a few motels around Amsterdam, and most surrounding towns and villages boast at least one hotel, where accommodation will be clean, quiet, friendly, and probably 30 per cent cheaper than its counterpart in the big city.

Single rooms, when available, cost 30 to 40 per cent less than a double. Service charges and tax are included in the rates, but normal tipping of staff is customary.

Youth hostels *(jeugdherberg).* The authorities encourage young people not to sleep rough. The addresses and prices of cheap accommodation—including youth hostels—are given in the above-mentioned hotel list. Otherwise, you can call Nederlandse Jeugdherbergcentrale, Prof. Tulpplein 4, Amsterdam, tel. 55 13 155.

a single room	**een eenpersoonskamer**
a double room	**een tweepersoonskamer**
with/without bath	**met/zonder bad**
What's the rate per night?	**Wat is het tarief per nacht?**

H **HOURS.** All city banks are open from 9 a.m. to 4 p.m., Monday to Friday, and Thursday also from 4.30 to 7 p.m. You can change money 24 hours a day, seven days a week, at the exchange office of 'Grens-wisselkantoren' (GWK) in the Central Station.

The N.Z. Voorburgwal post office is open Monday to Friday from 8.30 a.m. to 6 p.m. (Thursday, till 8.30 p.m.) and on Saturday mornings from 9 to noon. The Oosterdokskade branch has slightly longer hours: Monday to Friday, 8.30 a.m. to 9 p.m. and Saturday mornings from 9 till noon.

The VVV office at Stationsplein 10 (opposite the Central Station) is open daily from 9 a.m. to 11 p.m. in July and August. Between September and Easter, hours are 9 a.m. to 6 p.m. Monday to Friday (5 p.m. on Saturday), and from 10 a.m. to 1 p.m. and 2 to 5 p.m. Sundays. From Easter to July, hours are 9 a.m. to 11 p.m. Monday to Saturday, to 9 p.m. Sundays.

Consulates normally open from 9.30 or 10 a.m. to noon and from 2 or 2.30 to 4 or 5 p.m.

L **LANGUAGE.** The Dutch have a talent for languages, and you'll virtually never need to feel cut off because of problems of communication. English and German are widely understood and spoken, and French is a good runner-up. For politeness' sake, don't forget to inquire "Do you speak English?" before asking a question.

Do you speak English?	**Spreekt u Engels?**
Good morning	**Goedemorgen**
Good afternoon	**Goedemiddag**
Good evening	**Goedenavond**
Please/Thank you	**Alstublieft/Dank u**
You're welcome	**Tot uw dienst**
Goodbye/See you later	**Dag/Tot ziens**

The Berlitz phrase book DUTCH FOR TRAVELLERS covers most situations you're likely to encounter in your travels in Holland and Dutch-speaking Belgium. The Berlitz Dutch-English/English-Dutch pocket dictionary contains a 12,500-word glossary of each language, plus a menu-reader supplement.

LAUNDRY and DRY-CLEANING *(wasserij; stomerij).* The large hotels offer same-day service (but not on Saturdays, Sundays and 116 holidays). Laundromats *(wassserette),* laundries and dry-cleaners are

easy to find, and their prices are considerably lower than those
charged by hotels.

When will it be ready?	**Wanneer is het klaar?**
I must have this for	**Ik heb dit morgenvroeg**
tomorrow morning.	**nodig.**

LOST AND FOUND PROPERTY *(gevonden voorwerpen);* **LOST CHILDREN.** For general lost-property enquiries, telephone the police at 559 80 05. For the public-transport lost-property office, telephone 551 49 11. For property lost in taxis, telephone 77 77 77. For property lost at Schiphol Airport, telephone 649 14 33. For property left on planes, phone the airport police tel. 601 23 25. If you lose something on a train, ring 557 85 44.

If your child has wandered away, mobilize the first Dutch person you can find—your hotel receptionist, the girl at the department store counter, or a passer-by. You may have to go to the local police station, though it's more likely that you'll soon find your child being well looked after by an English-speaking Dutch person.

| I've lost my wallet/ | **Ik ben mijn portefeuille/** |
| handbag/passport/child. | **handtas/paspoort/kind kwijt.** |

MAPS *(kaart).* Road maps of the Netherlands are on sale at filling stations as well as in bookshops. Very detailed, indexed street plans of Amsterdam and the other main Dutch cities are produced by Falk-Verlag, Hamburg, which also prepared the maps in this guide.

| a street plan of Amsterdam | **een plattegrond van Amsterdam** |
| a road map of this region | **een wegenkaart van deze streek** |

MEDICAL CARE. See also EMERGENCIES. Medical insurance covering foreign travel is a wise investment. See your travel agent or regular insurance company about it.

For most residents of the United Kingdom, reciprocal agreements with the Netherlands ensure that a substantial proportion of emergency medical costs incurred in Holland will be reimbursed. Procedure, which must be strictly observed, is set out in leaflet SA 28 and forms E 111 and CM 1 available from Social Security offices. Travel agents offer supplementary insurance—a worthwhile precaution in view of the high cost of medical treatment in Holland.

M   Prescriptions are made up at an *apotheek* (chemist's shop or drugstore). There are always a few on night and weekend duty, the addresses are displayed at every chemist's. You can also telephone 664 21 11 (the same number will advise about emergency doctors or dentists). English and German are widely spoken in medical circles.

a doctor/a dentist	**een arts/een tandarts**
an ambulance	**een ziekenauto**
hospital	**ziekenhuis**
an upset stomach	**maagstoornis**
a fever	**koorts**
Where's the chemist on duty?	**Is er een apotheek in de buurt, die dienst heeft?**

MEETING PEOPLE. Despite the apparent "anything-goes" attitude, Amsterdammers are quite formal at heart. A handshake on meeting and departure is *de rigueur,* and a pleasant *dag meneer* ("good-day, sir") or *dag mevrouw* ("good-day, madam") is appreciated as a greeting at almost any time of day. It can be repeated upon parting, together with *tot ziens,* a familiar way of saying "goodbye" or "see you later". "Please" is *alstublieft,* also used in the sense of 'here you are', and "thank you" *dank u.*

MONEY MATTERS. The unit of Dutch currency is the *gulden,* usually called the guilder, or more rarely the florin, in English. It's abbreviated *f, fl, gld.* or *DFL.,* and is divided into 100 *cents* (abbreviated *c*). Coins include 5, 10 and 25 cents and 1, 2½ and 5 guilders. Banknotes come in denominations of 5, 10, 25, 50, 100, 250 and 1,000 guilders.

Banks *(bank).* All city banks will exchange foreign money. See also HOURS.

Currency-exchange offices *(wisselkantoor).* You can change money 24 hours a day at the exchange office of 'Grenswisselkantoren' (GWK) in Central Station. There are also numerous exchange points throughout the centre which stay open till late at night, but beware—they often charge an exorbitant commission without warning.

Credit cards *(credit card).* All major hotels and many restaurants and shops will accept payment by credit card.

Traveller's cheques *(reischeque)*. These are widely accepted, if you have passport identification.

I want to change some pounds/dollars.	**Ik wil wat ponden/dollars wisselen.**
Do you accept traveller's cheques?	**Accepteert u reischeques?**
Can I pay with this credit card?	**Kan ik met deze credit card betalen?**

NEWSPAPERS and MAGAZINES *(krant; tijdschrift)*. Many major foreign newspapers and magazines are available at shops and newsstands throughout the centre of Amsterdam, at hotels and at the airport. London papers will be there from early morning, and for Americans in particular there's the Paris-based *International Herald Tribune*, with latest U.S. stock reports and world news. *Holland Herald*, a backgrounder to Amsterdam and Dutch life, published monthly in Amsterdam in English only, is also a available from central newsstands.

Have you any English-language newspapers?	**Heeft u Engelstalige kranten?**

PHOTOGRAPHY. Developing and printing are of high quality. Numerous one-hour services exist but they are more expensive than normal developing, which will take a couple of days. For black-and-white films, you might have to wait a week.

Using a flash is forbidden in most museums, and in some the camera is banned altogether. Check with the attendant, if he has not already checked you. It may not be quite the same, but good reproductions (transparencies, postcards, prints) are available at all museums.

I'd like a film for this camera.	**Mag ik een film voor dit toestel?**
black-and-white film	**een zwart-wit film**
colour film for slides	**een kleurenfilm voor dia's**
How long will it take to develop (and print) this film?	**Hoe lang duurt het ontwikkelen (en afdrukken) van deze film?**

POLICE *(politie)*. In Amsterdam you'll see policemen and policewomen patrolling on foot as well as cruising in white Volkswagens.

P When trouble occurs, these cars will converge like bees on a hive. City police are dressed soberly in navy blue, with peaked caps, and are courteous to tourists.

The emergency police telephone number (but emergency *only*) is 22 22 22. For general enquiries, call city headquarters *(hoofdbureau)* at Elandsgracht 117, telephone 559 91 11. There are also district stations dotted around town showing a prominent POLITIE sign.

Where's the nearest police station?	**Waar is het dichtstbijzijnde politiebureau?**

PRICES. See also page 104. To keep costs down, avoid the big hotels and try the many cosy, neighbourhood bars for a drink. Local liquors such as the different *jenevers* will also save you a fortune compared to imported Scotch. If breakfast isn't included in your hotel room rate, you'll certainly get it cheaper at one of the city's scores of sandwich shops *(broodjeswinkels)*.

If you're out for the night-life, the discos and small clubs charge no entrance fee but upgrade the drinks in proportion to what is being offered in the way of music, dancing and other attractions. Don't forget a guilder for the cloakroom attendant, and one or two for the doorman, on the way out.

BTW is the abbreviation for the Dutch sales tax, the equivalent of the British VAT. It's nearly always included in purchases, rentals, meals, etc. *(inclusief BTW).*

If you make any expensive buys in Holland, enquire at the point of sale whether tax is included and, if so, whether it could be redeemed at customs upon your departure from the country. Diamond merchants and others accustomed to selling to tourists will be acquainted with the necessary procedures to be followed.

How much is it?	**Hoeveel kost het?**
Have you something cheaper?	**Heeft u iets goedkopers?**
Can we have VAT deducted?	**Kunnen we de BTW aftrekken?**

PUBLIC HOLIDAYS *(openbare feestdag).* Though Holland's banks, offices and major shops close on the country's eight public holidays, most museums will still be open from 1 to 5 p.m., and it's 120 business as usual in the restaurants and tourist-oriented domains.

January 1	*Nieuwjaar*	New Year's Day
April 30	*Koninginnedag*	Queen's Birthday
December 25 and 26	*Kerstfeest*	Christmas Day and Boxing Day
Movable dates:	*Goede Vrijdag*	Good Friday
	Tweede Paasdag	Easter Monday
	Hemelvaartsdag	Ascension Thursday
	Tweede Pinksterdag	Whit Monday

PUBLIC TRANSPORT. An extensive network of buses *(bus)*, trams *(tram)* and underground/subway *(metro)* lines comes to life around 6 a.m. and continues till shortly after midnight. Thereafter night buses *(nachtbus)* serve a number of key routes, usually at half-hourly intervals.

Holland, for the purposes of local and regional bus, tram and subway travel, is divided into some 2,000 zones, of which Amsterdam forms six. Fares are therefore calculated in zones corresponding with strips on the 'Nationale strippenkaart', valid throughout the country. Tickets are obtainable from: the tram or bus driver (day tickets, 3- and 10-strip tickets, which are more expensive); at metro stations (automatic ticket dispensers for day tickets and for single trips of one, two, three or four zones); at post offices, at railway stations and at many tobacconists (for 15-strip tickets). Tickets include transfer to other bus, tram or metro lines.

Stamp your ticket in the yellow stamping machine (for trams, at the rear; for buses, left of the front door; for the metro, near the stairs leading to the platforms); and *always* use one strip more than the number of zones you are crossing.

If you are planning to spend a day in Amsterdam, buy a day ticket *(dagkaart)*, valid for one day and the next night, entitling you to unlimited rides on any of the city's public transport systems. Two-day or three-day tickets are also available, but they can only be obtained at the GVB ticket booth *(kaartverkoop)* in front of the Central Station and at the GVB head office at Prins Hendrikkade 108 (near Central Station).

For further information, telephone 27 27 27.

RADIO and TV *(radio; televisie)*. The BBC is easily picked up in Holland. For music-lovers, excellent programmes are broadcast from the local Hilversum stations.

R All British and American films and series are shown on TV in their original language with Dutch subtitles. Amsterdam has cable television, which enables programmes to be seen from neighbouring countries.

RELIGIOUS SERVICES *(kerkdienst).* In Amsterdam, Sunday services in English are held in the following churches:

Catholic: Catholic church in the Begijnhof

Protestant: English Reformed Church in the Begijnhof
               Christ Church (Church of England), Groenburgwal 42
               Christian Centre Fellowship, Euromotel, Oude Haagse Weg

Jewish services are held in the synagogues at Jacob Obrechtsplein and Lekstraat 61. In summer, it's possible to attend services at the famous 17th-century Portuguese synagogue near Waterlooplein (tel. 22 61 88).

T **TAXIS** *(taxi).* They are recognized by a taxi sign on the roof. Generally they do not cruise the streets looking for fares, but return after a job to one of their ranks. If you do spot one with the roof-sign lit, it means the cab is free, and you can hail it. You can phone for a taxi, either by calling the radio-controlled *taxicentrale* (77 77 77) or your nearest rank. A novelty is the "Treintaxi", which operates in 30 towns and takes passengers from the railway station to any place within the municipal boundaries or vice versa for only *f* 5.

Most places of interest in Amsterdam can also be reached by **water taxi** (75 09 09). Boats take up to eight passengers, plus luggage and bicycles. Fares are shared.

What's the fare to...?   **Hoeveel kost het naar...?**

TIME DIFFERENCES. The following chart shows the time differences between Holland and various cities in winter. In summer, Dutch clocks are put forward one hour.

New York	London	**Amsterdam**	Jo'burg	Sydney	Auckland
6 a.m.	11 a.m.	**noon**	1 p.m.	10 p.m.	midnight

TIPPING. Service is included in hotel and restaurant bills. It is customary to round off taxi fares and leave a few coins for the waiter in restaurants. Some further suggestions:

Hotel porter, per bag	ƒ 2
Maid, per week	ƒ 15
Lavatory attendant	50 cts.
Cinema/Theatre usher	50 cts.–ƒ 1
Hairdresser/Barber	included
Tourist guide	5–10%

TOILETS *(toiletten).* There's a lack of public lavatories in Amsterdam, but the hundreds of café-bars are designated as public places and you may use their toilet facilities. It would seem polite to have a beer or a coffee on the way out. Most department stores have smart, clean, public toilets, usually with an attendant on duty. Be sure to put a coin in the waiting saucer, or you may learn a few new Dutch expressions.

Where are the toilets?   **Waar zijn de toiletten?**

TOURIST INFORMATION OFFICES. Netherlands Board of Tourism (National Bureau voor Toerisme) offices, at the addresses given below, will help you when planning your trip.

Australia: 6th floor, 5 Elizabeth St., Sydney, NSW 2000; tel. 02-276-921

British Isles: 25–28 Buckingham Gate, London SW1E 6LD; tel. (071) 630-0451

Canada: 25 Adelaide St. East, Suite 710, Toronto, Ont. M5C 1Y2; tel. (416) 363-1577

U.S.A.: 355 Lexington Ave., New York, NY 10017; tel. (212) 370-7367 255 N. Michigan Ave., Suite 326, Chicago, IL 60601; tel. (312) 819-0300 90 New Montgomery Street, Suite 305, San Francisco, CA 94105; tel. (415) 543-6772

In individual Dutch towns, tourist affairs are handled by an office of a separate organization known universally by its abbreviation VVV (pronounced vay-vay-vay). Blue signs bearing the triple-V guide you to the tourist office from the edge of any town.

Amsterdam's VVV offices are at Stationsplein 10, opposite Central Station (tel. 26 64 44) and in Leidsestraat 106.

Where is the tourist office?	**Waar is het VVV-kantoor?**

TRAINS *(trein)*. Dutch trains run on time. It's a matter of national pride. Services are excellent. From Amsterdam you can be in Haarlem in 14 minutes and in The Hague in 45. Other destinations are equally well provided for.

There are special one-day, eight-day and monthly ticket offers.

The information bureau at Central Station is open daily (see HOURS). Take one of the tickets there that assures your rightful place in the "queue". Alternatively, telephone 06-899 11 21 (NS-Infocentrum) or, for information on international trains, 20 22 66.

WATER *(water)*. No worries at all (though the native Amsterdammer swears it's not as good as it used to be). Drink it—it's perfectly safe.

A glass of water, please.	**Een glaasje water, alstublieft.**

NUMBERS

0	**nul**	15	**vijftien**
1	**een**	16	**zestien**
2	**twee**	17	**zeventien**
3	**drie**	18	**achttien**
4	**vier**	19	**negentien**
5	**vijf**	20	**twintig**
6	**zes**	21	**eenentwintig**
7	**zeven**	30	**dertig**
8	**acht**	40	**veertig**
9	**negen**	50	**vijftig**
10	**tien**	60	**zestig**
11	**elf**	70	**zeventig**
12	**twaalf**	80	**tachtig**
13	**dertien**	90	**negentig**
14	**veertien**	100	**honderd**

SOME USEFUL EXPRESSIONS

yes/no	**ja/nee**
please/thank you	**alstublieft/dank u**
excuse me/you're welcome	**pardon/tot uw dienst**
where/when/how	**waar/wanneer/hoe**
how long/how far	**hoelang/hoever**
yesterday/today/tomorrow	**gisteren/vandaag/morgen**
day/week/month/year	**dag/week/maand/jaar**
left/right	**links/rechts**
large/small	**groot/klein**
open/closed	**open/dicht**
old/new	**oud/nieuw**
up/down	**boven/beneden**
hot/cold	**warm/koud**
Do you speak English?	**Spreekt u Engels?**
I don't understand.	**Ik begrijp het niet.**
Please write it down.	**Wilt u het opschrijven, alstublieft?**
What does this mean?	**Wat betekent dit?**
Help me, please.	**Help mij, alstublieft.**
Get a doctor—quickly!	**Haal een doktor—vlug!**
What time is it?	**Hoe laat is het?**
How much is it?	**Hoeveel kost het?**
It's urgent.	**Het is dringend.**
Waiter!/Waitress!	**Ober!/Juffrouw!**
I'd like…	**Ik wil graag…**

DAYS

Sunday	**zondag**
Monday	**maandag**
Tuesday	**dinsdag**
Wednesday	**woensdag**
Thursday	**donderdag**
Friday	**vrijdag**
Saturday	**zaterdag**

Index

An asterisk (*) next to a page number indicates a map reference. For index to Practical Information, see inside front cover.

Selection of
Hotels and
Restaurants
in
Amsterdam and
The Hague

BERLITZ

Where do you start? Choosing a hotel or restaurant in a place you're not familiar with can be difficult. To give you some initial help, we have made a few selections from the *Red Guide to Benelux* published by Michelin, the recognized authority on gastronomy and accommodation throughout Europe.

Our own Berlitz criteria have been price and location. In the hotel section, for a double room with bath and breakfast, Higher-priced means above f 350, Medium-priced f 175–350, Lower-priced below f 175. As to restaurants, for a meal consisting of a starter, a main course and a dessert, Higher-priced means above f 80, Medium-priced f 50–80, Lower-priced below f 50. For restaurants in the section called "Outside Amsterdam", however, to avoid confusion of detail, we have simply replaced the three categories with $$$ for Higher-priced, $$ for Medium-priced and $ for Lower-priced. Special features where applicable, plus regular closing days are also given. For hotels and restaurants, both a check to make certain that they are open and advance reservations are advisable. In Amsterdam, a booking service is available at Schiphol airport and at the VVV tourist information centre on Stationsplein opposite the Central Station. In The Hague, there is a VVV centre in the main station.

For a wider choice of hotels and restaurants, we strongly recommend you obtain the authoritative Michelin *Red Guide to Benelux*, which gives a comprehensive and reliable picture of the situation throughout these countries.

BENELUX

AMSTERDAM

HOTELS

HIGHER-PRICED (above f350)

Central Amsterdam

American
Leidsekade 97
1017 PN Amsterdam
Tel. 624 5322
Tlx. 11379
186 rooms. Café Américain restaurant. Outdoor dining.

Amstel
Professor Tulpplein 1
1018 GX Amsterdam
Tel. 622 6060
Tlx. 11004
111 rooms. Shady terrace overlooking the Amstel. La Rive restaurant.

Amsterdam Marriott
Stadhouderskade 21
1054 ES Amsterdam
Tel. 683 5151
Tlx. 15087
395 rooms. All modern comforts. Port O'Amsterdam restaurant.

Europe
Nieuwe Doelenstraat 2
1012 CP Amsterdam
Tel. 623 4836
Tlx 12081
100 rooms. All modern comforts. View. Indoor swimming pool. Excelsior restaurant.

Grand Hotel Krasnapolsky
Dam 9
1012 JS Amsterdam
Tel. 554 9111
Tlx. 12262
330 rooms. Le Reflet d'Or and Edo (Japanese) restaurants.

Pulitzer
Prinsengracht 323
1016 GZ Amsterdam
Tel. 523 5235
Tlx. 16508
246 rooms. De Goudsbloem restaurant.

Sonesta
Kattengat 1
1012 SZ Amsterdam
Tel. 621 2223
Tlx. 17149
425 rooms. All modern comforts. Rib Room restaurant.

Victoria
Damrak 1
1012 LG Amsterdam
Tel. 623 4255
Tlx. 16625
160 rooms. Van Riebeeck restaurant.

South and West Amsterdam

Amsterdam Hilton
Apollolaan 138
1077 BG Amsterdam
Tel. 678 0780
Tlx. 11025
261 rooms. All modern comforts. Kei Japanese restaurant. Terrace restaurant.

Sander
Jacob Obrechtstraat 69
1071 KJ Amsterdam
Tel. 662 7574
Tlx. 18456
16 rooms. No restaurant.

LOWER-PRICED (below *f175*)

Central Amsterdam

Asterisk
Den Texstraat 16
1017 ZA Amsterdam
Tel. 626 2396
19 rooms. No restaurant.

Engeland
Roemer Visscherstraat 30a
1054 EZ Amsterdam
Tel. 612 9691
28 rooms. No restaurant.

Fantasia
Nieuwe Keizersgracht 16
1018 DR Amsterdam
Tel. 623 8259
19 rooms.

Linda
Stadhouderskade 131
1074 AW Amsterdam
Tel. 662 5668
17 rooms. No restaurant.

Nicolaas Witsen
Nicolaas Witsenstraat 6
1017 ZH Amsterdam
Tel. 626 6546
31 rooms. No restaurant.

Owl Hotel
Roemer Visscherstraat 1
1054 EV Amsterdam
Tel. 618 9484
Tlx. 13360
34 rooms. No restaurant.

Parklane
Plantage Parklaan 16
1018 ST Amsterdam
Tel. 622 4804
11 rooms.

De Roode Leeuw
Damrak 93
1012 LP Amsterdam
Tel. 620 5875
76 rooms.

Sipermann
Roemer Visscherstraat 35
1054 EW Amsterdam
Tel. 616 1866
13 rooms. No restaurant.

Vondel
Vondelstraat 28
1054 GE Amsterdam
Tel. 612 0120
23 rooms.

South and West Amsterdam

Borgmann
Koningslaan 48
1075 AE Amsterdam
Tel. 673 5252
15 rooms. No restaurant.

Fita
Jan Luykenstraat 37
1071 CL Amsterdam
Tel. 679 0976
20 rooms. No restaurant.

Savoy
Michelangelostraat 39
1077 BR Amsterdam
Tel. 679 0367
Tlx. 18970
13 rooms. No restaurant.

Toro
Koningslaan 64
1075 AG Amsterdam
Tel. 673 7223
12 rooms. Quiet situation.
No restaurant.

Wilhelmina
Koninginneweg 169
1075 CN Amsterdam
Tel. 662 5467
Tlx. 10873
16 rooms. No restaurant.

Zandbergen
Willemsparkweg 205
1071 HB Amsterdam
Tel. 676 9321
Tlx. 33756
17 rooms. No restaurant.

Schiphol Airport

HIGHER-PRICED

Hilton International Schiphol
Herbergierstraat 1
1118 ZK Amsterdam
Tel. (020) 511 5911
Tlx. 15186
282 rooms. All modern comforts.
Indoor swimming pool.

MEDIUM-PRICED

Barbizon Schiphol
Kruisweg 495
2132 NA Hoofddorp
Tel. (02503) 64422
Tlx. 74546
248 rooms. All modern comforts.
De Meerlanden restaurant.

RESTAURANTS

HIGHER-PRICED (above *f80*)

Central Amsterdam

De Cost Gaet Voor De Baet Uyt
1st floor
Oude Brugsteeg 16
1012 JP Amsterdam
Tel. 624 7050
View. Closed Saturday lunchtime
and Sunday.

Dikker en Thijs
Prinsengracht 444
Corner with Leidsestraat
1017 KE Amsterdam
Tel. 625 8876
Tlx. 13161
Dinner only. Open till midnight.
Closed Sunday. 25 rooms.

Dynasty
Reguliersdwarsstraat 30
1017 BM Amsterdam
Tel. 626 8400
Oriental. Dinner only. Outdoor
dining. Closed Tuesday.

Excelsior
H. Europe
Nieuwe Doelenstraat 2
1012 CP Amsterdam
Tel. 623 4836
Tlx. 12081
Notably good cuisine.
Elegant restaurant. View.
Closed Saturday lunchtime.

Les Quatre Canetons
Prinsengracht 1111
1017 JJ Amsterdam
Tel. 624 6307
Closed lunchtime Saturday
and Sunday.

't Swarte Schaep
1st floor
Korte Leidsedwarsstraat 24
1017 RC Amsterdam
Tel. 622 3021
17th-century interior decor.

South and West Amsterdam

Het Bosch
Jollenpad 10
1081 KC Amsterdam
Tel. 644 5800
View. Outdoor dining.
Pleasant lakeside terrace.
Closed Sunday Oct.–March.

De Kersentuin
Garden H.
Dijsselhofplantsoen 7
1077 BJ Amsterdam
Tel. 664 2121
Tlx. 15453
Notably good cuisine.
Closed Saturday lunchtime
and Sunday.

Parkrestaurant Rosarium
Europaboulevard
Amstelpark 1
1083 HZ Amsterdam
Tel. 644 4085
Set in flowered park. Outdoor
dining in summer. Closed Sunday.

Trechter (de Wit)
Hobbemakade 63
1071 XL Amsterdam
Tel. 671 1263
Notably good cuisine.
Closed Sunday and Monday.
Dinner only.

MEDIUM-PRICED (*f50–80*)

Central Amsterdam

Albatros
Westerstraat 264
1015 MT Amsterdam
Tel. 627 9932
Seafood specialities. Dinner only.
Closed Sunday.

Bols Taverne
Rozengracht 106
1016 NH Amsterdam
Tel. 624 5752
Closed Saturday lunchtime
and Sunday.

La Camargue
Reguliersdwarsstraat 7
1017 BJ Amsterdam
Tel. 623 9352

Christophe
Leliegracht 46
1015 DH Amsterdam
Tel. 625 0807
Notably good cuisine. Dinner only. Closed Sunday.

Da Canova
Warmoesstraat 9
1012 HT Amsterdam
Tel. 626 6725
Italian cuisine. Dinner only. Closed Sunday and Monday.

De Gijsbrecht van Aemstel
Herengracht 435
1017 BR Amsterdam
Tel. 626 2500
Rustic restaurant-taverna. Closed Sunday.

Lana-Thai
Warmoesstraat 10
1012 JD Amsterdam
Tel. 624 2179
Thai cuisine.

Manchurian
Leidseplein 10a
1017 PT Amsterdam
Tel. 626 2105
Oriental cuisine.

Martinn
12th floor
De Ruyterkade 7 (havengebouw)
1013 AA Amsterdam
Tel. 625 6277
Closed Saturday and Sunday. View.

Mirafiori
Hobbemastraat 2
1071 ZA Amsterdam
Tel. 622 3013
Italian cuisine. Closed Tuesday.

Oesterbar
Leidseplein 10
1017 PT Amsterdam
Tel. 626 3463
Seafood specialities.

Le Pêcheur
Reguliersdwarsstraat 32
1017 BM Amsterdam
Tel. 624 3121
Seafood specialities. Outdoor dining. Closed lunchtime Saturday and Sunday.

Pied de Cochon
Noorderstraat 19
1017 TR Amsterdam
Tel. 623 7677
Dinner only.

Prinsenkelder
Prinsengracht 438
1017 KE Amsterdam
Tel. 626 7721
Dinner only.

Sancerre
Reestraat 28
1016 DN Amsterdam
Tel. 627 8794

't Seepaerd
1st floor
Rembrandtsplein 22
1017 CV Amsterdam
Tel. 622 1759
Seafood specialities. Outdoor dining. Open till midnight.

Sichuan Food
Reguliersdwarsstraat 35
1017 BK Amsterdam
Tel. 626 9327
Chinese cuisine. Dinner only. Closed Wednesday.

De Silveren Spiegel
Kattengat 4
1012 SZ Amsterdam
Tel. 624 6589
*Closed Saturday lunchtime
and Sunday.*

Sjef Schets
Leidsestraat 20
1017 PA Amsterdam
Tel. 622 8085
*Outdoor dining. Closed Saturday
lunchtime and Sunday.*

Tout Court
Runstraat 13
1016 GJ Amsterdam
Tel. 625 8637
Dinner only.

Les Trois Neufs
Prinsengracht 999
1017 KM Amsterdam
Tel. 622 9044
Closed Monday.

South and West Amsterdam

Beddington's
Roelof Hartstraat 6
1071 VH Amsterdam
Tel. 676 5201
Closed Saturday and Sunday.

Brasserie Van Baerle
Van Baerlestraat 158
1071 BG Amsterdam
Tel. 679 1532
Outdoor dining. Closed Saturday.

De Castheele
Kastelenstraat 172
1082 EJ Amsterdam
Tel. 644 7267
Closed Sunday and Monday.

Henri Smits
Beethovenstraat 55
1077 HN Amsterdam
Tel. 679 1706
Closed Sunday lunchtime.

In den Nederhoven
Nederhoven 13
1083 Am Amsterdam
Tel. 642 5619
*Outdoor dining. Closed Saturday
and Sunday lunchtime.*

Keyzer
Van Baerlestraat 96
1071 BB Amsterdam
Tel. 671 1441
Closed Sunday.

LOWER-PRICED (below ƒ50)

Central Amsterdam

Bistro La Forge
Korte Leidsedwarsstraat 26
1017 RC Amsterdam
Tel. 624 0095
Dinner only. Open till midnight.

La Cacerola
Weteringstraat 41
1017 SM Amsterdam
Tel. 626 5397
*Spanish cuisine. Dinner only.
Closed Sunday.*

Corneille
Herenstraat 25
1015 BZ Amsterdam
Tel. 638 0148
*Dinner only. Closed Sunday
and Monday.*

De Groene Lanteerne
Haarlemmerstraat 43
1013 EJ Amsterdam
Tel. 624 1952
Traditional Dutch interior.
Closed Sunday and Monday.

Haesje Claes
Spuistraat 273
1012 RV Amsterdam
Tel. 624 9998
Closed Sunday lunchtime.

Holland's Glorie
Kerkstraat 222
1017 GV Amsterdam
Tel. 624 4764
Dinner only.

Indonesia
1st floor
Singel 550
1017 AZ Amsterdam
Tel. 623 1758
Indonesian cuisine.

Kopenhagen
Rokin 84
1012 KX Amsterdam
Tel. 624 9376
Danish specialities.
Closed Sunday.

Koriander
Amstel 212
1017 AH Amsterdam
Tel. 627 7879
View. Dinner only. Open till
midnight. Closed Sunday and
Monday.

Lotus
Binnen Bantammerstraat 5
1011 CH Amsterdam
Tel. 624 2614
Chinese cuisine. Dinner only.
Closed Saturday.

Lucius
Spuistraat 247
1012 VP Amsterdam
Tel. 624 1831
Seafood. Dinner only.

Mandarijn
Rokin 26
1012 KS Amsterdam
Tel. 623 0885
Chinese cuisine.

Mangerie
Spuistraat 3b
1012 SP Amsterdam
Tel. 625 2218
Dinner only. Outdoor dining.

Selecta
Vijzelstraat 26
1017 HK Amsterdam
Tel. 624 8894
Indonesian cuisine.

Treasure
Nieuwe Zijds Voorburgwal 115
1012 RH Amsterdam
Tel. 626 0915
Chinese cuisine.

South and West Amsterdam

L'Arena
Olympiaplein 105
1077 CT Amsterdam
Tel. 679 0435
Italian cuisine. Closed Saturday
and Sunday lunchtime.

Croq-O-Vin
Stadionweg 100
1077 SR Amsterdam
Tel. 671 1119
Closed Sunday.

Les Fréres
Bosboom Toussaintstraat 70
1054 AV Amsterdam
Tel. 618 7905
Dinner only. Closed Sunday.

La Grande Bouffe
le Constantijn Huygensstraat 115
1054 BV Amsterdam
Tel. 618 8191
Dinner only. Closed Saturday.

Hamilcar
Overtoom 306
1054 JC Amsterdam
Tel. 683 7981
Tunisian cuisine. Dinner only.
Closed Monday.

Miranda Paviljoen
Amsteldijk 223
1079 LK Amsterdam
Tel. 644 5768

Oriënt
Van Baerlestraat 21
1071 AN Amsterdam
Tel. 673 4958
Indonesian cuisine.
Closed Saturday and Sunday
lunchtime.

Ravel
Gelderlandplein 2
1082 LA Amsterdam
Tel. 644 1643
Taverna. Closed Sunday lunch-
time.

Sama Sebo
P.C. Hooftstraat 27
1071 BL Amsterdam
Tel. 662 8146
Indonesian cuisine. Closed
Sunday.

OUTSIDE AMSTERDAM

$$$ = Higher-priced
$$ = Medium-priced
$ = Lower-priced

Aviorama $$
3rd floor
Schipholweg 1
1118 AA Amsterdam
Tel. 604 1105
At the airport. View.

De Boekanier $$$
Oude Haagseweg 49
1066 BV Amsterdam
Tel. 617 3525
Near A4 highway to Den Haag.
Outdoor dining.
Closed Saturday and Sunday.

Het Kampje $$
Kerkstraat 56
1191 JE Ouderkerk aan de
Amstel
Tel. (02963) 1943
Outdoor dining. Closed
Wednesday, Saturday and
Sunday.

Klein Paardenburg $$$
Amstelzijde 59
1184 TZ Ouderkerk aan de
Amstel
Tel. (02963) 1335
Notably good cuisine. Outdoor
dining. Closed Saturday
lunchtime, Sunday and
Monday.

De Meerpaal $$
Noordeinde 78a
1121 AG Amsterdam
Tel. (02908) 3381
*In Landsmeer. Closed Saturday
and Sunday lunchtime.*

Molen De Dikkert $$$
Amsterdamseweg 104a
1182 HG Amstelveen
Tel. (020) 411378
*Notably good cuisine. Pleasant
elegant restaurant in converted
17th-century mill, Closed Saturday lunchtime and Sunday.*

Paardenburg $$$
Amstelzijde 55
1184 TZ Ouderkerk aan de
Amstel
Tel. (02963) 1210
*19th-century murals.
Waterside terrace.
Closed Sunday.*

Rôtisserie Ile de France $$$
Pieter Lastmanweg 9
1181 XG Amstelveen
Tel. (020) 453509
*Good cuisine. Closed Saturday
lunchtime, Sunday and Monday.*

Gekroonde Hamer $$
Breestraat 24
2011 ZZ Haarlem
Tel. (023) 312243
*Dinner only. Outdoor dining.
Closed Sunday.*

Hilda $
Wagenweg 214
2012 NM Haarlem
Tel. (023) 312871
*Indonesian cuisine. Dinner only.
Closed Saturday and Sunday
lunchtime and Monday.*

DEN HAAG

HOTELS

HIGHER-PRICED

Des Indes
Lange Voorhout 54
2514 EG Den Haag
Tel. (070) 469553
Tlx. 31196
67 rooms.

Scheveningen

Kurhaus
Gevers Deijnootplein 30
2586 CK Scheveningen
Tel. (070) 520052
Tlx. 33295
*249 rooms. View. Ground-floor
casino. Kandinsky restaurant.*

MEDIUM-PRICED

Bel Air
Johan de Wittlaan 30
2517 JR Den Haag
Tel. (070) 502021
Tlx. 31444
*350 rooms. Indoor swimming
pool.*

Corona
Buitenhof 42
2513 AH Den Haag
Tel. (070) 637930
Tlx. 31418
26 rooms. Notably good cuisine.

Paleis Hotel
Molenstraat 26
2513 BL Den Haag
Tel. (070) 624621
Tlx. 34349
20 rooms. No restaurant.

Parkhotel Den Haag
Molenstraat 53
2513 BJ Den Haag
Tel. (070) 624371
Tlx. 33005
124 rooms. No restaurant.

Promenade
Van Stolkweg 1
2585 JL Den Haag
Tel. (070) 525161
Tlx. 31162
99 rooms. Elegant hotel
with collection of modern paintings.
Cigogne restaurant.

Sofitel
Koningin Julianaplein 35
2595 AA Den Haag
Tel. (070) 814901
Tlx. 34001
144 rooms. All modern comforts.

Scheveningen

Carlton Beach Hotel
Gevers Deijnootweg 201
2586 HZ Scheveningen
Tel. (070) 541414
Tlx. 33687

100 rooms. All modern comforts.
View. Outdoor dining.
Le Homard restaurant.
Indoor swimming pool.

Europa Hotel
Zwolsestraat 2
2587 VJ Scheveningen
Tel. (070) 512651
Tlx. 33138
174 rooms. Indoor swimming pool.
New Orleans Ribhouse restaurant.

LOWER-PRICED

Scheveningen

Badhotel
Gevers Deijnootweg 15
2586 BB Scheveningen
Tel. (070) 512221
Tlx. 31592
96 rooms.

RESTAURANTS

HIGHER-PRICED

Radèn Ajoe
Lange Poten 31
2511 CM Den Haag
Tel. (070) 644592
Indonesian cuisine.
Closed Sunday lunchtime.

Da Roberto
Noordeinde 196
2514 GS Den Haag
Tel. (070) 464977
*Italian cuisine. Closed Saturday
and Sunday lunchtime and
Tuesday.*

Saur
Lange Voorhout 51
2514 EC Den Haag
Tel. (070) 463344
*Notably good cuisine. Seafood
specialities. Closed Saturday
lunchtime and Sunday.*

Scheveningen

Radèn Mas
Gevers Deijnootplein 125
2586 CX Scheveningen
Tel. (070) 545432
*Indonesian cuisine.
Closed Sunday lunchtime.*

Seinpost (Savelberg)
Zeekant 60
2586 AD Scheveningen
Tel. (070) 555250
Notably good cuisine. View.

MEDIUM-PRICED

Aubergerie
Nieuwe Schoolstraat 19
2514 HT Den Haag
Tel. (070) 648070
Dinner only. Closed Tuesday.

Le Gobelet
Noordeinde 143
2514 GG Den Haag
Tel. (070) 465838
*Open till midnight. Closed
Sunday.*

La Grande Bouffe
Maziestraat 10
2514 GT Den Haag
Tel. (070) 654274
*Closed Saturday and Sunday
lunchtime and Monday.*

Jean Martin
Groenewegje 115
2515 LP Den Haag
Tel. (070) 802895
*Dinner only. Closed Sunday and
Monday.*

Julien
Vos in Tuinstraat 2a
2514 BX Den Haag
Tel. (070) 658602
*Open till midnight. Closed
Saturday and Sunday lunchtime.*

Roma
Papestraat 22
2513 AW Den Haag
Tel. (070) 462345
*Italian cuisine. Closed Sunday
lunchtime and Tuesday.*

Royal Dynasty
Noordeinde 123
2514 GG Den Haag
Tel. (070) 652598
Thai cuisine. Closed Monday.

Table du Roi
Prinsestraat 130
2513 CH Den Haag
Tel. (070) 461908
*Dinner only. Closed Monday
and Tuesday.*

Scheveningen

Le Bon Mangeur
Wassenaarsestraat 119
2586 AM Scheveningen
Tel. (070) 559213
*Dinner only. Closed Sunday
and Monday.*

China Delight
Dr Lelykade 118
2583 CN Scheveningen
Tel. (070) 555450
Chinese cuisine.

Ducdalf
Dr Lelykade 5
2583 CL Scheveningen
Tel. (070) 557692
Seafood specialities.

La Galleria
Gevers Deijnootplein 120
2586 CP Scheveningen
Tel. (070) 521176
Italian cuisine. Outdoor dining.

LOWER-PRICED

Brasserie Pastel
1st floor
Laan van Roos en Doorn 51a
2514 BC Den Haag
Tel. (070) 643750
Dinner only.

't Goude Hooft
1st floor
Groenmarkt 13
2513 AL Den Haag
Tel. (070) 469713

Le Gourmand
Breitnerlaan 84
2596 HD Den Haag
Tel. (070) 241782
Closed Sunday.

De Verliefde Kreeft
Bleijenburg 11
2511 VC Den Haag
Tel. (070) 644522
*Seafood.
Closed Saturday and
Sunday lunchtime.*

Scheveningen

Bali
Badhuisweg 1
2587 CA Scheveningen
Tel. (070) 502434
*Indonesian cuisine. Dinner only.
34 rooms.*

De Goede Reede
Dr Lelykade 236
2583 CP Scheveningen
Tel. (070) 548820
*Closed Saturday and Sunday
lunchtime.*